Writing in the Disciplines
Advice and Models

A Hacker Handbooks Supplement

Jonathan S. Cullick
Northern Kentucky University

Terry Myers Zawacki
George Mason University

D0291007

BEDFORD/ST. MARTIN'S
Boston ◆ New York

DISCIPLINE SPECIALISTS

For their assistance and advice as discipline specialists, we thank the following: Diana Belland, Northern Kentucky University (music); Jules Benjamin, Ithaca College (history); Dorinda J. Carter, Michigan State University (education); Jennifer DeForest, University of Virginia (education); Susan Durham, George Mason University (nursing); C. Dale Elifrits, Northern Kentucky University (geology/engineering); Aimee Frame, University of Cincinnati (engineering); Devon Johnson, George Mason University (criminal justice); Victoria McMillan, Colgate University (biology); James Morris, Harvard University (biology); Kirsten Olson, Wheaton College (education); Shannon Portillo, George Mason University (criminal justice); Sherry Robertson, Arizona State University (business); and Beth Schneider, George Mason University (business).

Printed in the United States of America.

1 0 9 8 7 6
f e d c b a

For information, write: Bedford/St. Martin's, 75 Arlington Street, Boston, MA 02116   (617-399-4000)

ISBN 978-1-319-08354-0

ACKNOWLEDGMENTS

Jules Benjamin, "Wage Slavery or True Independence? Women Workers in the Lowell, Massachusetts, Textile Mills, 1820–1850," excerpt from *A Student's Guide to History*, Eleventh Edition. Copyright © 2010 by Bedford/St. Martin's. Reprinted with permission.

Valerie Charat, "Always Out of Their Seats (and Fighting): Why Are Boys Diagnosed with ADHD More Often Than Girls?" (December 15, 2006). Reprinted with permission.

Onnalee L. Gibson, "A Reflection on Service Learning: Working with Eric" (April 25, 2006). Reprinted with permission.

Tom Houston, "Concert Review" (February 27, 2008). Reprinted with permission.

Marin Johnson and Laura Arnold, "Distribution Pattern of Dandelion (*Taraxacum officinale*) on an Abandoned Golf Course" (September 13, 2005). Reprinted with permission.

Victoria McMillan, excerpt from *Writing Papers in the Biological Sciences*, Fourth Edition. Copyright © 2006 by Bedford/St. Martin's. Reprinted with permission.

Alice O'Bryan, "Site Stabilization Plan for Erosion Control" (May 5, 2008). Reprinted with permission.

Kelly Ratajczak, "Proposal to Add a Wellness Program" (April 21, 2006). Reprinted with permission.

Julie Riss, "Acute Lymphoblastic Leukemia and Hypertension in One Client: A Nursing Practice Paper" (May 18, 2006). Reprinted with permission.

Brian Spencer, "Positively Affecting Employee Motivation" (March 9, 2006). Reprinted with permission.

Chris Thompson, "Crime in Leesburg, Virginia." Reprinted with permission.

Writing in the
Disciplines

Advice and Models

D Writing in the Disciplines

D1 Introduction: Writing in different disciplines

Succeeding in college requires performing well in different kinds of courses and on various kinds of assignments. You know you will be assigned writing in your college writing courses, but it may surprise you to know that other college courses require writing—courses you might not expect, like nursing and psychology. The strategies you develop in your first-year composition course will help you write well in other academic courses.

The academic community is divided into broad subject areas called *disciplines*. The disciplines are generally grouped into five major fields of study, which are further broken down into more specific subjects. The five disciplines and a few representative subjects are social sciences (psychology, sociology, criminology); natural sciences (biology, physics, chemistry); mathematics and engineering; humanities and the arts (history, literature, music); and professions and applied sciences (business, education, nursing).

Each discipline has its own set of expectations and conventions for both reading and writing. Some of the expectations and conventions—writing with a clear main idea, for instance—are common across disciplines; those are covered in your handbook. Other expectations and conventions are unique to each discipline. These include the following:

- purpose for writing
- audience
- questions asked by scholars and practitioners
- types of evidence used
- language and writing conventions
- citation style

When you are asked to write in a specific discipline, start by becoming familiar with the distinctive features of writing in that discipline. For example, if you are asked to write a lab report for a biology class, your purpose might be to present results of an experiment. Your evidence would be the data you collected while conducting your experiment, and you would use scientific terms in your report. You would also use the CSE (Council of Science Editors) guidelines for citation of your sources. If you are asked to write a case study for an education class, your purpose might be to analyze student-teacher interactions in a classroom. Your evidence might be data on a combination of personal observations and interviews. You would use terms from the field in your case study and cite your sources using the guidelines of the American Psychological Association (APA).

The following sections provide guidelines for writing in nine disciplines: biology, business, criminal justice/criminology, education, engineering, history, music, nursing, and psychology. Each section begins with advice about the expectations for writing in that discipline and closes with a model or two of student writing.

D2 Writing in the biological sciences

Biologists use writing in many ways. They write reports analyzing the data they collect from their experiments as well as reviews of other scientists' research or proposed research. They write proposals to convince funding agencies to award grants for their research. If they teach, biologists also write lectures. Some biologists may communicate with a general audience by writing newspaper and magazine articles. In addition, they may lend their expertise to public-policy decision making by government officials, weighing in on, say, the issue of global warming or stem cell research.

When you write in biology courses, your goal will generally be to convince readers of the validity of the conclusions you draw from observations, from experimental data, or from your evaluations of previously published or proposed research. For most assignments, you will need to use a scientific style of writing, conveying your information to readers as succinctly and accurately as possible.

D2-a Determine your audience and their needs in the biological sciences.

When you write in biology, your audience may consist of researchers, professors, other students, and sometimes members of the government or business communities and the general public. Researchers or teachers may read to find out the results of an experiment, an analysis of new data, or information supporting or critiquing a theory. They may need this information to guide their own research projects or improve their assignments and classroom materials. Students read to learn about major concepts and discoveries as well as methods for conducting laboratory experiments. Researchers, teachers, and students expect detailed, specific presentation of data and findings in words and in graphic form, such as diagrams and graphs. Members of the general public want to understand how concepts affect personal decisions they must make about issues such as medical care or nutritional choices. People working in government or business may have to make decisions about funding for research proposals. For more general audiences, you may not need to provide the same level of detail. For example, the public or businesspeople may not need species names to be written in Latin. In all cases, however, your readers expect you to be completely objective and to present information as clearly as possible.

D2-b   Recognize the forms of writing in the biological sciences.

When you take courses in biology, you may be asked to write any of the following:

- laboratory notebooks
- research papers
- laboratory reports
- literature reviews
- research proposals
- poster presentations

Laboratory notebooks

If you are required to complete laboratory exercises, you will need to carefully record your experiments in a notebook. A laboratory notebook should be detailed and accurate so that anyone who wishes to repeat your experiment can do so. The laboratory notebook also provides crucial material for any report or article you may write later about your experiment. Researchers take notebooks seriously, never removing a page or erasing entries. That practice keeps them from misrepresenting results.

Your notebook will typically have the following components:

- table of contents
- date of each experiment
- title
- purpose (the objective of the experiment)
- materials (a list of equipment, specimens, and chemicals you used in the experiment)

- procedures (the method you planned to follow as well as any alterations you made to that procedure while conducting the experiment)
- results (the data gathered from the experiment)
- data analysis (calculations based on your data)
- discussion (your assessment of whether the experiment was successful, your interpretation of your results, your accounting for any surprising results, and your conclusions about what you learned from the experiment)
- acknowledgments (those who helped you with the experiment)

Research papers and laboratory reports

When instructors refer to *research papers*, they may have different assignments in mind. One assignment might ask you to present your synthesis of many sources of information about, for instance, a genetic syndrome to demonstrate your understanding of the characteristics of the disorder and other researchers' investigations of the causes of the syndrome.

Another assignment might require you to report on the results of an experiment you conducted and to interpret your results; this document is typically called a *laboratory report*. Unlike the laboratory notebook, a lab report may relate your interpretations to what others in the field have concluded from their own experiments. Biologists publish research papers and reports in journals after the papers have undergone rigorous and impartial review by other biologists, called a *peer review*, to make sure that the scientific process used by the researchers is sound.

Whether published in a journal or written for a college course, research papers and reports based on original experiments follow a standard format and include the following sections:

- abstract (a 100-to-125-word summary of your report)
- introduction (the context for your experiment, such as what has been published on the topic in the field, as well as the purpose of the experiment)
- materials and methods (details of how you conducted the experiment so that other researchers can repeat the experiment to try to reproduce your results; your description of the methodology you used so that readers can determine if your interpretations are supported by the data)
- results (a presentation of what you observed in the experiment)
- figures and tables

- discussion (your interpretation of the results as well as a comparison of your interpretation and that of other researchers in the field)
- references (a list of the sources cited in your paper)

Literature reviews

Literature reviews can have different objectives, such as comparing or contrasting approaches to a problem or examining the literature in the field to propose an alternative theory. Another purpose is to inform biologists about the latest advances in the field. In a review, you will consider the findings of a number of research papers and evaluate those papers' conclusions and perhaps suggest a direction for future research. A critical review analyzes the methods and interpretations of data from one or more journal articles. You may be asked to write a literature review as an introduction to a larger piece of writing, such as a report of a study you conducted. In that case, the review will survey previously published findings relevant to the question that your study investigates.

A literature review assignment is an opportunity to learn about an area in the field and to see what old or new questions may benefit from research.

While the format of reviews varies with their purpose, reviews typically have an abstract, an introduction, a discussion of the research being reviewed, a conclusion, and a references section.

Research proposals

In a research proposal, the biologist poses a significant question and a hypothesis (or hypotheses) and suggests one or more experiments to test the hypothesis. The project can have specific practical applications; for example, one Arctic biologist submitted to the United States Geological Survey a proposal for an ecological monitoring program at a national park. Research proposals that seek funding for an experiment must include detailed budgets.

Whether written by scholars requesting support from an agency or by students in a course, research proposals are evaluated for how well they justify their project with a carefully conceived experiment design.

Poster presentations

At professional gatherings such as annual conventions in the field, biologists have the opportunity to present their work in the form of a poster rather than as a formal talk. Conference attendees approach presenters in an exhibit area to talk about their research, which the posters concisely summarize. A poster features a brief introduction to the presenter's research project, a description of the method, information about the experiment's subjects, the experiment's results, and the presenter's conclusions. Poster presentations also feature graphs and tables since it is important to convey information to attendees quickly and concisely as they walk through the exhibit area. An effective poster presentation will encourage the audience to ask questions and carry on an informal conversation with the presenter.

Your instructor may ask you to create a poster presentation about an experiment you or other researchers have conducted both to help you understand complex concepts and to practice your communication skills.

NOTE: Some presenters use presentation software to create a slide show that they can click through for a small audience or project on a screen for a larger group. Presenters generally include the same kinds of information in slide presentations as they do in poster presentations.

D2-c Know the questions biologists ask.

Biologists, like other scientists, ask questions about the natural world. Their questions are either *why* questions or *how* questions, such as the following:

- Why don't newborns see well?
- Why does body size of species skew to the right on a distribution curve? That is, why are there so many small animals?
- How does cellular senescence prevent cancer?
- How do island plants self-pollinate?

As they attempt to answer such questions, biologists first offer a tentative explanation, or hypothesis, for something they have observed. They perform an experiment to test their hypothesis. If the results from the experiment match the original predictions, then they consider the hypothesis supported, but not proved, since biologists cannot account for all conditions. Other biologists will continue to formulate new hypotheses and offer new findings.

D2-d Understand the kinds of evidence biologists use.

Biologists use many kinds of evidence:

- data from site studies or site surveys
- observations of specimens with the aid of special equipment, such as a microscope

- observations and measurements made in experimental settings
- data taken from reports that other biologists have published

Data in biology, which are either quantitative (that which can be counted) or qualitative (that which can be described without numbers), can take various forms, depending on the nature of the site, the type of experiment, or the specialized field in which the research is performed. Following are some examples.

- For a study of the mating choices of female swordfish, biologists might record and analyze responses from females placed in tanks with males.
- In forensic biology, researchers might interpret the data they collect from tests on criminal suspects' DNA samples.
- Plant biologists might analyze the rates of survival of native tree seedlings affected by chemicals released by invasive plant species.

Because evidence can have more than one plausible interpretation, biologists offer alternative explanations for the results obtained in experiments. For example, the authors of one article suggested that differences in the type and availability of prey could account for why Atlantic blue marlin larvae grew faster in one body of water than in another, but they also recognized that other possible causes related to differences in spawning populations.

D2-e Become familiar with writing conventions in the biological sciences.

Biologists agree on several conventions when they write.

- Scientific writing often uses the passive voice to describe how a researcher has performed an experiment (*Blue marlin larvae were collected*). The passive voice can be useful for drawing attention to the action itself, not to who has performed the action. But biologists use the active voice whenever possible to convey information clearly and efficiently (*Researchers collected blue marlin larvae*). With the use of the active voice, the first-person pronouns *I* and *we* are acceptable, even preferred, if the passive voice creates awkward-sounding sentences and adds unnecessary words.
- Direct quotation of sources is rare; instead, biologists paraphrase to demonstrate their understanding of the source material and to convey information economically.

- Biologists use the past tense to describe the materials and methods and the results of their own experiments.

- Biologists use the present tense to describe the published findings of other studies.

- Biologists often include specific scientific names for species (*Canis latrans* for the coyote, for instance).

D2-f   Use the CSE system for citing sources.

Biologists typically use the style recommended by the Council of Science Editors (CSE) to format their paper, to cite sources in the text of the paper, and to list the sources at the end. The CSE describes three citation systems in *Scientific Style and Format: The CSE Manual for Authors, Editors, and Publishers*, 8th ed. (Chicago: CSE, 2014). In the *name-year* system, the author's last name and the date of publication are cited in the text. In the *citation-sequence* system, each source is assigned a number the first time it is used in the text, and the same number identifies the source each time it appears. In the *citation-name* system, each source is assigned a number in the order in which it appears in the alphabetical list at the end of the paper. That number is used each time the source is cited in the text.

With all three systems, biologists place bibliographic information for each source at the end of the paper in a section called References or Cited References.

D2-g   Sample student paper: Laboratory report

Conducting an experiment gives you practice in collecting and interpreting data. Writing a laboratory report allows you to describe an experiment and its results. The following laboratory report was written for a botany course. The writers used the style guidelines of the Council of Science Editors (CSE) for formatting their paper and citing and listing sources in the citation-sequence system.

Distribution Pattern of Dandelion

(*Taraxacum officinale*)

on an Abandoned Golf Course

Title page consists of a descriptive title and the writers' names in the center of the page and the course, instructor, and date centered at the bottom of the page.

Marin Johnson

Laura Arnold

Lab 4

Botany 100A

Professor Ketchum

September 13, XXXX

Marginal annotations indicate CSE-style formatting and effective writing.

Distribution Pattern of Dandelion 2

ABSTRACT

This paper reports our study of the distribution pattern of the
common dandelion (*Taraxacum officinale*) at an abandoned golf course
in Hilton, NY, on 10 July 2005. An area of 6 ha was sampled with 111
randomly placed 1×1 m^2 quadrats. The dandelion count from each
quadrat was used to test observed frequencies against expected frequencies
based on a hypothesized random distribution. We concluded that the
distribution of dandelions was not random. We next calculated the
coefficient of dispersion to test whether the distribution was aggregated
(clumped) or uniform. The calculated value of this coefficient was
greater than 1.0, suggesting that the distribution was aggregated. Such
aggregated distributions are the most commonly observed types in natural
populations.

An abstract
summarizes the
report in about
100–125 words.
You may or may
not be required
to include an
abstract with a
brief lab report.

INTRODUCTION

Theoretically, plants of a particular species may be aggregated
(clumped), random, or uniformly distributed in space.[1] The distribution
type may be determined by many factors, such as availability of nutrients,
competition, distance of seed dispersal, and mode of reproduction.[2]

The purpose of this study was to determine if the distribution
pattern of the common dandelion (*Taraxacum officinale*) on an abandoned
golf course was aggregated, random, or uniform.

Introduction states
the purpose of the
experiment.

Citations are
numbered in the
order in which they
appear in the text
(citation-sequence
system).

METHODS

The study site was an abandoned golf course in Hilton, NY. The
vegetation was predominantly grasses, along with dandelions, broad-leaf
plantain (*Plantago major*), and bird's-eye speedwell (*Veronica chamaedrys*).
We sampled an area of approximately 6 ha on 10 July 2005, approximately
two weeks after the golf course had been mowed.

To ensure random sampling, we threw a tennis ball high in the air
over the study area. At the spot where the tennis ball came to rest, we
placed one corner of a 1×1 m^2 metal frame (quadrat). We then counted
the number of dandelion plants within this quadrat. We repeated this
procedure for a total of 111 randomly placed quadrats.

We used a two-step procedure.[2] We first tested whether the distribution
of dandelion was random or nonrandom. From the counts of the number of
dandelions in our 111 quadrats, we used a log-likelihood ratio

The writers use
scientific names for
plant species.

Detailed description
of researchers'
methods.

(*G*) test to examine the goodness of fit between our observed frequencies and those expected based on the Poisson series $e^{-\mu}$, $\mu e^{-\mu}$, $\mu^2/2!e^{-\mu}$, $\mu^3/3!e^{-\mu}$, . . . , where μ is the mean density of plants per quadrat. In carrying out this test, we grouped observed and expected frequencies so that no group had an expected frequency less than 1.0.[3] We then determined whether the distribution was aggregated or uniform by calculating the coefficient of dispersion (ratio of the variance to the mean). A coefficient > 1 indicates an aggregated distribution whereas a coefficient < 1 indicates a more uniform distribution. Finally, we tested the significance of any departure of the ratio from a value of 1 by means of a *t*-test.

Header contains a short title and the page number.

Specialized language of the field.

RESULTS

Table 1 shows the number of quadrats containing 0, 1, 2, . . . , 17 dandelion plants. More than two-thirds (67.6%) of the 111 quadrats contained no dandelion plants; almost 90% (89.2%) of the quadrats contained fewer than 3 dandelion plants. We observed a highly significant lack of fit between our observed frequencies and expected frequencies based on the Poisson distribution ($G = 78.4$, df $= 3$, $P < 0.001$). Thus, our data indicated that the distribution pattern of dandelion plants on the abandoned golf course was not random. The mean number of dandelion plants per quadrat was 1.05 (SD $= 2.50$), and the coefficient of dispersion was 5.95. A *t*-test showed that this value is significantly greater than 1.0 ($t = 36.7$, df $= 110$, $P < 0.001$), which strongly supports an aggregated distribution of the dandelion plants.

Headings organize the report into major sections.

DISCUSSION

An aggregated (clumped) distribution is the most commonly observed distribution type in natural populations.[4] Among plants, aggregated distributions often arise in species that have poorly dispersed seeds or vegetative reproduction.[2] In the dandelion, the seeds are contained in light, parachute-bearing fruits that are widely dispersed by the wind. This method of seed dispersal would tend to produce a random distribution. However, dandelion plants also reproduce vegetatively by producing new shoots from existing taproots, and what we considered as groups of closely spaced separate individuals probably represented

Writers interpret their results and compare them with results of other researchers.

Distribution Pattern of Dandelion 4

Table presents the data collected by the researchers in an accessible format.

Table 1 Frequency distribution of dandelion (*Taraxacum officinale*) plants in 1×1 m^2 quadrats positioned randomly over 6 ha on an abandoned golf course

Nr per quadrat	Observed frequency (f_i)	Expected frequency (f_i)[a]
0	75	38.68594
1	12	40.77707
2	12	21.49062
3	2	7.550757
4	3	1.989727
5	2	0.419456
6	0	0.073688
7	2	0.011096
8	0	0.001462
9	1	0.000171
10	0	1.8×10^{-5}
11	0	1.73×10^{-6}
12	0	1.52×10^{-7}
13	1	1.23×10^{-8}
14	0	9.27×10^{-10}
15	0	6.52×10^{-11}
16	0	4.29×10^{-12}
17	1	2.66×10^{-13}
Total 111		

[a] Expected frequencies were calculated from the successive terms of the Poisson distribution (see Methods).

shoots originating from the same plant. Thus, vegetative reproduction probably accounted for the observed aggregated distribution in this species.

REFERENCES

Sources are listed and numbered in the order in which they appear in the text.

1. Ketchum J. Lab manual for Botany 100; 2005.

2. Kershaw KA, Looney JHH. Quantitative and dynamic plant ecology. 3rd ed. London: Edward Arnold; 1985.

3. Zar JH. Biostatistical analysis. 5th ed. Englewood Cliffs (NJ): Prentice Hall; 2005.

4. Begon M, Harper JL, Townsend CR. Ecology: individuals, populations and communities. Oxford: Blackwell Science Limited; 1996.

D3 Writing in business

Communication, especially writing, is central to the business world. Because business writers generally aim to persuade or inform their audiences, they place a premium on clarity, brevity, and focus. When you write in business courses, your goal will be to communicate in a straightforward manner and with a clear purpose.

D3-a Determine your audience and their needs in business.

When you write in business, your audience may be varied. One type of audience might be executives, managers, and employees in various departments of a company—accounting, research and development, sales, and clerical support. Another audience might consist of stockholders, clients, and potential customers. Audiences within a business organization read to consider proposals for revising existing products, services, projects, policies, or procedures or for creating new ones. Business owners and executives may read to gather information to help them evaluate projects in progress, to assess sales, and to make decisions about changing product designs or adopting new marketing strategies. They read to understand whether a course of action would be feasible and profitable for the business. Managers, salespeople, and other employees read memos, e-mail, and other documents to help them conduct the daily transactions and activities of the organization, solve daily problems, and respond to customers. Customers read the publications of a business to learn about products and services and to determine whether it would benefit them to do business with a particular company.

For all of your readers, present empirical data such as sales figures or cost structures in easily readable formats such as tables, charts, and graphs. It might also be appropriate to give your readers opinions from questionnaires or surveys. A business owner deciding whether to adopt a marketing strategy might want to read feedback from potential customers, and a potential customer might want to read testimonials from satisfied customers. Respect your readers' time. Make sure your writing is clear, straightforward, focused, attractively presented on paper or a Web site, and as brief as possible. Because trust is essential in business transactions, maintain a respectful tone and project a credible image. Business writing should make personal connections and use inclusive language.

D3-b   Recognize the forms of writing in business.

In business courses, you will be asked to create documents that mirror the ones written in professional settings. The different forms of business writing covered in this section are used for varied purposes, such as informing and persuading. Assignments in business courses may include the following:

- reports
- proposals
- executive summaries
- memos and correspondence
- presentations
- brochures, newsletters, and Web sites

Reports

Reports present factual information for a variety of purposes. If your company is considering the development of a new product, you may be asked to write a feasibility report that lays out the pros and cons. If you are asked to determine how your sales compare with those of a competitor, you will need to write an investigative report. A progress report updates a client or supervisor about the status of a project. A formal report details a major project and generally requires research.

Proposals

Proposals are written with the goal of convincing a specific audience to adopt a plan. A solicited proposal is directed to an audience that has requested it. An unsolicited proposal is written for an audience that has not indicated interest. An internal proposal is directed at others within an organization. An external proposal is directed at clients or potential clients. The length of a proposal will vary depending on your goals and your intended audience.

Executive summaries

An executive summary provides a concise summary of the key points in a longer document, such as a proposal or a report, with the goal of drawing the reader's attention to the longer document.

Memos and correspondence

In business, communication often takes place via letter, memo, or e-mail. Letters and e-mail are written to clients, customers, and colleagues. Memos convey information to others in the same organization for a variety of purposes. A memo might summarize the results of a study or project, describe policies or standards, put forth a plan, or assign tasks.

Presentations

Presentations are usually done orally, in front of a group, to instruct, persuade, or inform. Presenters often use presentation software or tools such as whiteboards to prepare and display visuals—graphs, tables, charts, transparencies, and so on.

Brochures, newsletters, and Web sites

Brochures generally convey information about products or services to clients, donors, or consumers. Newsletters generally provide information about an organization to clients, members, or subscribers. Web sites may either advertise products or provide information about an organization.

D3-C Know the questions business writers ask.

In business, your purpose and your understanding of your audience will determine the questions you ask.

- If you are writing a proposal to persuade a client to adopt a product, you will ask, "How will this product benefit my client?" and "What does my client need?"
- If you are asked to write a report informing your supervisor of your progress on a project, you will ask, "What does my supervisor need to know to authorize me to proceed?" You will also want to ask, "What does my supervisor already know?" and "How can I target this report to address my supervisor's specific concerns?"
- If you are applying for a job, you will ask, "What qualifications do I have for this job?"

D3-d Understand the kinds of evidence business writers use.

In business, your purpose for writing, your audience, and the questions you ask will determine the type of evidence you use. The following are some examples of the way you might use evidence in business writing.

- If you are writing a report or a proposal, you may need to gather data through interviews, direct observation, surveys, or questionnaires. The sources of data you choose will be determined by your audience. For example, if you are studying the patterns of customer traffic at a supermarket to recommend a new layout, you might go to the supermarket and observe customers or you might ask them to fill out surveys as they leave the store. If your audience is the store manager, you might focus on surveys at one store. If your audience is the owner of a large grocery chain, you would probably need to use data from several stores.

- If you are writing an investigative report in which you consider how to entice users to a health club, your evidence might include facts and statistics about the health benefits of exercise that you have drawn from published materials such as books, articles, and reports. You might also conduct research about the facilities of a competitor. In a long proposal or report, your evidence will probably come from a variety of sources rather than just one source.

- If you are applying for a job, your evidence will be your past experience and qualifications. For example, you might explain that you have worked in the industry for six years and held three management positions. You might also discuss how the skills you learned in those jobs will be transferable to the new position.

- If you are writing a brochure to promote a service, your evidence might be testimonials from satisfied users of the service. For example, a brochure advertising nanny services might quote a customer who says, "We found a full-time nanny who is both experienced and energetic—a perfect fit for our family."

D3-e Become familiar with writing conventions in business.

In business, writing should be straightforward and professional, but not too formal.

- Buzzwords (*value-added*, *win-win*, *no-brainer*) and clichés (*The early bird catches the worm*) should be used sparingly. This kind of vocabulary is imprecise and can sound phony or insincere.

- Use personal pronouns such as *you* and *I*. Where appropriate (in letters, e-mail, proposals), you can use the pronoun *you* to emphasize the interests of your readers. When you are addressing multiple readers, you might want to avoid using *you* unless it is clear that you are referring to all readers. When you are expressing your opinion, you should use the pronoun *I*. When you are speaking on behalf of your company, you should use the pronoun *we*.

- It is important to avoid language that could offend someone on the grounds of race, gender, sexual orientation, or disability. Use terms like *chair* or *chairperson* instead of *chairman* or *chairwoman*. Unless it is relevant to your point, avoid describing people by race or ethnicity. If you are describing someone with a disability, use phrases like *client with a disability* rather than *disabled client* to show that you recognize the disability as one trait rather than as a defining characteristic of the person. (Also see "appropriate language" in your handbook.)

- Business writing should always be concise. Avoid using words that are not essential to your point. Instead of writing *at this point in time*, just write *now*. Also avoid words that make a simple idea unnecessarily complicated. Using the passive voice often creates such complications. Instead of writing *This report was prepared to inform our customers*, write *We prepared this report to inform our customers*.

D3-f Use the APA or CMS (*Chicago*) system in business writing.

Business students typically use the style guidelines of the American Psychological Association (APA) or *The Chicago Manual of Style* (CMS) for formatting their paper, for citing sources in the text of their paper, and for listing sources at the end. The APA system is set forth in the *Publication Manual of the American Psychological Association*, 6th ed. (Washington, DC: APA, 2010). CMS style is found in *The Chicago Manual of Style*, 16th ed. (Chicago: University of Chicago Press, 2010). (For more details, see the documentation sections in your handbook.) In business courses, instructors will usually indicate which style they prefer.

D3-g Sample student papers: An investigative report and a proposal

Sample report

Different business situations require different types of reports. Formal reports are comprehensive discussions of a topic from multiple angles, while investigative reports often focus on a specific issue. If you are asked to write a report, you should always be sure that you understand the expectations of your audience.

The investigative report beginning on page D-21 was written for an introductory course in business writing. The student, Brian Spencer, was asked to research the problem of employee motivation at a small company. He used the style guidelines of the American Psychological Association (APA) to format the paper and to cite and list sources.

Sample proposal

Proposals are written to convince a specific audience to adopt a plan. If you are asked to write a proposal, you might start by identifying the purpose and the audience for the document.

The internal proposal beginning on page D-28 was written for a course in business writing. The student, Kelly Ratajczak, wrote her proposal in the form of a memorandum to the senior vice president of human resources at the medium-size company where she completed an internship. Her goal was to convince the vice president to adopt a wellness program for employees.

SAMPLE REPORT

Positively Affecting Employee Motivation

Prepared by Brian Spencer

Report Distributed March 9, XXXX

Prepared for OAISYS

The title page of
a business report
is counted in
the numbering,
although a header
and page number
do not appear.

Title, writer's name,
and date, centered
on page; company
name, centered at
bottom.

Marginal annotations indicate business-style formatting and effective writing.

In a typical business report, the page header contains an abbreviated title and the page number.

Employee Motivation 2

Abstract

Corporate goals, such as sales quotas or increases in market share, do not always take into account employee motivation. Motivating employees is thus a challenge and an opportunity for firms that want to outperform their competitors. For a firm to achieve its goals, its employees must be motivated to perform effectively.

Empirical research conducted with employees of a subject firm, OAISYS, echoed theories published by leading authorities in journals, books, and online reports. These theories argue that monetary incentives are not the primary drivers for employee motivation. Clear expectations, communication of progress toward goals, accountability, and public appreciation are common primary drivers. A firm aiming to achieve superior performance should focus on these activities.

Abstract, on a separate page, provides a brief summary of the report.

While not strictly APA style, the formatting of the business report is consistent with the style typically used in business. Headings are flush with the left margin and boldface. Paragraphs are separated by an extra line of space, and the first line of each paragraph is not indented.

Employee Motivation 3

Introduction

All firms strive to maximize performance. Such performance is typically
defined by one or more tangible measurements such as total sales, earnings
per share, return on assets, and so on. The performance of a firm is created
and delivered by its employees. Employees, however, are not necessarily
motivated to do their part to maximize a firm's performance. Factors that
motivate employees can be much more complex than corporate goals. This
report will define the problem of employee motivation in one company and
examine potential solutions.

OAISYS is a small business based in Tempe, Arizona, that manufactures
business call recording products. Currently OAISYS employs 27 people. The
business has been notably successful, generating annual compound sales
growth of over 20% during the last three years. The company's management
and board of directors expect revenue growth to accelerate over the coming
three years to an annual compound rate of over 35%. This ambitious
corporate goal will require maximum productivity and effectiveness from all
employees, both current and prospective. OAISYS's management requested
an analysis of its current personnel structure focused on the alignment of
individual employee motivation with its corporate goal.

Background on Current Human Resources Program

OAISYS is currently structured departmentally by function. It has teams
for research and development, sales, marketing, operations, and
administration. Every employee has access to the same employment
benefits, consisting of medical insurance, a 401(k) plan, flexible spending
accounts, short- and long-term disability insurance, and the like.

Members of the sales team receive a yearly salary, quarterly commissions
tied to sales quotas, and quarterly bonuses tied to the performance of
specific tasks. These tasks can change quarterly to maintain alignment with
strategic initiatives.

All employees not in the sales department receive a yearly salary and
profit sharing at the end of the year. The formula for profit sharing is not

Introduction clearly presents the problem to be discussed and sets forth the scope of the report.

Heading announces the purpose of each section.

known by the employees, and specific information about profits is infrequently communicated. When profitability is discussed, it is only in general terms. Key employees, as determined by the management, are given stock option grants periodically. This process is informal and very confidential.

Disconnect Between Company and Employees

One common assumption is that a human resources program such as OAISYS's should be the platform for motivation. But monetary compensation is not the only driver of employee motivation (Dickson, 1973). In fact, studies have found that other factors are actually the primary drivers of employee motivation. Security, career advancement, the type of work, and pride in one's company are actually the highest-rated factors in employee satisfaction (Accel TEAM, 2005).

Spencer presents evidence from research studies.

These conclusions drawn from the empirical research of others are supported by interviews conducted with current OAISYS employees. Justin Crandall, a current design engineer, stated that his primary motivation is the opportunity to work with leading-edge development tools to pursue results of the highest quality (personal communication, March 1, 2006). Crandall's strongest sense of frustration comes from a cluttered organizational structure because it restricts his ability to pursue innovative, high-quality results.

Spencer provides evidence from interviews with current employees.

Interviews are considered personal communication in APA style; they are cited in the text of the paper but not given in the reference list.

Todd Lindburg, the most senior design engineer on staff, had similar sentiments. His greatest motivator is the opportunity to create something lasting and important to the long-term success of the business (personal communication, March 2, 2006). Jack Wikselaar, vice president of sales, said he receives his strongest motivation from providing fulfilling job opportunities for others (personal communication, March 3, 2006).

These findings of what motivates employees tell only half the story. Other research (*Motivating*, 2006) suggests that businesses can actually demotivate employees through certain behaviors, such as the following:

Employee Motivation 5

- company politics
- unclear expectations
- unnecessary rules and procedures
- unproductive meetings
- poor communication
- toleration of poor performance

A list draws readers' attention to important information.

Doug Ames, manager of operations for OAISYS, noted that some of these issues keep the company from outperforming expectations: "Communication is not timely or uniform, expectations are not clear and consistent, and some employees do not contribute significantly yet nothing is done" (personal communication, February 28, 2006).

Recommendations

It appears that a combination of steps can be used to unlock greater performance for OAISYS. Most important, steps can be taken to strengthen the corporate culture in key areas such as communication, accountability, and appreciation. Employee feedback indicates that these are areas of weakness or motivators that can be improved. This feedback is summarized in Figure 1.

The author lays out recommendations for action. Some reports also include a Conclusions section.

A plan to use communication effectively to set expectations, share results in a timely fashion, and publicly offer appreciation to specific contributors will likely go a long way toward aligning individual motivation with corporate goals. Additionally, holding individuals accountable for results will bring parity to the workplace.

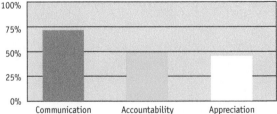

Figure 1. Areas of greatest need for improvements in motivation.

Graphic illustrates support for the report's key recommendation.

One technique that might be effective is basing compensation on specific responsibilities. Rather than tying compensation to corporate profit, tying it to individual performance will result in direct correlation between results and reward. Those who do what is necessary to achieve expected results will be rewarded. Those who miss the mark will be required to address the reasons behind their performance and either improve or take a different role. Professor of organizational behavior Jesper Sorenson (2002) has noted that "quantitative analyses have shown that firms with strong cultures outperform firms with weak cultures" (p. 70). Taking steps to strengthen the corporate culture is critical to the company's success.

Employee Motivation 7

References

Accel TEAM. (2005). *Employee motivation in the workplace*. Retrieved from
   http://www.accel-team.com/motivation

Dickson, W. J. (1973). Hawthorne experiments. In C. Heyel (Ed.), *The
   encyclopedia of management* (2nd ed., pp. 298-302). New York, NY:
   Van Nostrand Reinhold.

Motivating employees without money. (2006). Retrieved from http://www
   .employer-employee.com/howtomot.htm

Sorenson, J. B. (2002). The strength of corporate culture and the reliability
   of firm performance. *Administrative Science Quarterly*, *47*(1), 70-71.

Spencer provides a list of sources using APA style.

SAMPLE PROPOSAL

MEMORANDUM

Internal proposal is structured in memo format; subject is identified in the header.

To: Jay Crosson, Senior Vice President, Human Resources

From: Kelly Ratajczak, Intern, Purchasing Department

Subject: Proposal to Add a Wellness Program

Date: April 24, XXXX

Ratajczak opens with a clear, concise statement of her main point.

Health care costs are rising. In the long run, implementing a wellness program in our corporate culture will decrease the company's health care costs.

Introductory section provides supporting background information.

Research indicates that nearly 70% of health care costs are from common illnesses related to high blood pressure, overweight, lack of exercise, high cholesterol, stress, poor nutrition, and other preventable health issues (Hall, 2006). Health care costs are a major expense for most businesses, and they do not reflect costs due to the loss of productivity or absenteeism. A wellness program would address most, if not all, of these health care issues and related costs.

Headings clearly define the sections of the proposal.

Benefits of Healthier Employees

A wellness program would substantially reduce costs associated with employee health care, and in addition our company would prosper through many other benefits. Businesses that have wellness programs show a lower cost in production, fewer sick days, and healthier employees ("Workplace Health," 2006). Our healthier employees will help to cut not only our production and absenteeism costs but also potential costs such as higher turnover because of low employee morale.

While not strictly APA style, the memo format for a proposal is consistent with the style typically used in business. A header at the top of each page contains an abbreviated title and an arabic page number (the first page is counted in the numbering, although a number does not appear). Headings are flush with the left margin and boldface. Paragraphs are separated by an extra line of space, and the first line of each paragraph is not indented.

Implementing the Program

Implementing a good wellness program means making small changes to the work environment, starting with a series of information sessions. Simple changes to our work environment should include healthier food selections in vending machines and in the employee cafeteria. A smoke-free environment, inside and outside the building, could be a new company policy. An important step is to educate our employees through information seminars and provide health care guides and pamphlets for work and home. In addition, the human resources department could expand the current employee assistance program by developing online materials

Marginal annotations indicate business-style formatting and effective writing.

Wellness Program Proposal 2

that help employees and their families to assess their individual health
goals.

Each health program is different in its own way, and there are a number
of programs that can be designed to meet the needs of our individual
employees. Some programs that are becoming increasingly popular in
the workplace are the following ("Workplace Health," 2006):

- health promotion programs
- subsidized health club membership
- return-to-work programs
- health-risk appraisals and screenings

Obstacles: Individual and Financial

The largest barrier in a wellness program is changing the habits and
behaviors of our employees. Various incentives such as monetary bonuses,
vacation days, merchandise rewards, recognition, and appreciation help
to instill new habits and attitudes. Providing a healthy environment and
including family in certain programs also help to encourage healthier
choices and behaviors (Hall, 2006).

In the long run, the costs of incorporating a wellness program will be far
less than rising costs associated with health care. An employee's sense
of recognition, appreciation, or accomplishment is an incentive that has
relatively low or no costs. The owner of Natural Ovens Bakery, Paul Sitt,
has stated that his company gained financially after providing programs
including free healthy lunches for employees (Springer, 2005). Sitt said he
believes that higher morale and keeping valuable employees have helped
his business tremendously.

It is important that our company be healthy in every way possible.
Research shows that 41% of businesses already have some type of wellness
program in progress and that 32% will incorporate programs within the
next year ("Workplace Health," 2006). Our company should always be
ahead of our competitors. I want to thank you for your time, and I look
forward to discussing this proposal with you further next week.

*Ratajczak identifies
and responds to
potential concerns.*

*The concluding
paragraph
summarizes the
main point, provides
support for being
competitive,
and indicates a
willingness to
discuss the proposal.*

Wellness Program Proposal 3

References

Ratajczak provides
a list of sources,
formatted in APA
style.

Hall, B. (2006). Good health pays off! Fundamentals of health promotion

incentives. *Journal of Deferred Compensation 11*(2), 16-26. Retrieved

from http://www.aspenpublishers.com/

Springer, D. (2005, October 28). Key to business success? *La Crosse*

Tribune. Retrieved from http://lacrossetribune.com/

Workplace health and productivity programs lower absenteeism,

costs. (2006). *Managing Benefit Plans 6*(2), 1-4. Retrieved

from http://www.ioma.com/

D4 Writing in criminal justice and criminology

Criminal justice and criminology are part of the same broad field. Criminal justice refers to the application of policing practices and policies, and criminology is chiefly concerned with the theories that explain those practices and policies. The field of criminal justice and criminology draws from a diverse range of disciplines, including sociology, political science, public administration, psychology, history, and law. Holding this multidisciplinary field together is its fundamental focus on justice. Whatever your specialization as a student—policing, law enforcement management, juvenile justice, corrections, law and the courts, or homeland security—you may be asked to write papers on topics such as policing practices and policies, the administration of justice, legal decision making, and the theories criminologists use to explain and analyze crime. Your instructors may also ask you to imagine different audiences and purposes to prepare you for the wide range of readers and writing tasks you'll encounter in various workplaces.

D4-a Determine your audience and their needs in criminal justice and criminology.

Criminal justice professionals write for diverse audiences, including peers and supervisors in an organization or members of other, related organizations, readers of professional and academic publications, and the general public. When you write in a criminal justice course, you might be asked to imagine that you are writing a memo to a new police chief explaining local crime trends and demographics. Or you might write a memo to the head of a law enforcement organization describing a policing practice or policy and making recommendations for change. You might write about the same practice or policy for an audience of public defenders or for public resources officers who must make sure that citizens understand what the policy means to them. You might be asked to write an article about the practice or policy for a magazine such as *Police Chief*, whose audience consists of many different kinds of practitioners in the field. Given these multiple and often overlapping audiences, you must analyze your readers' needs carefully.

D4-b Recognize the forms of writing in criminal justice and criminology.

When you take courses in criminal justice and criminology, you may be asked to write in a variety of forms for diverse audiences and purposes. These forms include the following:

- research papers
- analytical papers
- argument or position papers
- investigative and administrative reports
- policy memos
- case briefs and legal briefs
- case plans (or case notes)

Research papers

A research paper in a criminal justice course requires you to identify an issue or a topic and then to research or explore the data that have been compiled about the topic (called *secondary sources*). You might also be expected to use *primary sources*—interviews or surveys that you conduct. In most cases, you'll be expected to find your own angle on the topic and to make an argument about it. You might also be required to apply a theory you've studied to your research findings. In a policing course, you might investigate whether police officers from different racial and ethnic backgrounds make decisions differently. To obtain information, you might conduct interviews and read published studies. In a social inequality and justice class, you might investigate whether the focus of racial profiling shifted from African Americans to Muslims after September 11, 2001, and what scholars are saying about possible trends. In a course on corrections, you might examine the punitive practice of solitary confinement and consider what this prison practice indicates about US law and society.

Analytical papers

Often you'll be given assignments that ask you to apply the theories you've studied to a situation, a legal case, or a personal account written by someone in the criminal justice system. For assignments like these, you will generally be expected to describe the theory and its main components and to use the theory to explain specific situations and people's behaviors and life choices. For example, you might be asked to analyze how discretionary theory applies to street-level policing or to critique a theory by comparing it with other theories that attempt to explain the same behaviors and choices. Sometimes analytical papers conclude with program or policy recommendations based on the usefulness or persuasiveness of the theory.

Argument or position papers

In argument or position papers, you are expected to present both sides of an issue in a balanced way and then to take a position. Your position will be based on your analysis of the course readings and lectures or on research you've conducted, not on your personal opinion. You might also be asked to compare or contrast relevant theories and cases to support your position. For example, an assignment might ask you to argue for more or less discretionary power for street-level policing, using as evidence cases in which that power has been used or abused. Or, after investigating trends in racial profiling, you might take a position supporting or opposing changes in the current policies. Or you might argue that the practice of long-term solitary confinement is or is not justified as a crime control approach in US penal policy.

Investigative and administrative reports

Law enforcement professionals and criminologists write both investigative and administrative reports. Some common investigative reports are crime and arrest reports, incident and accident reports, and presentencing reports. A typical crime or arrest report includes a clear timeline of events, for both the crime and the investigation, such as when the defendant was taken into custody, read his or her Miranda rights, and interviewed. The report should also include other details about the criminal investigation—for example, where the interview with the defendant took place, who else was present, and whether any other witnesses were interviewed. Administrative reports typically include a description of a problem, supported by research and statistical data, and recommendations based on an analysis of the data. A consultant's administrative report to a new police chief, for example, may include a briefing about the demographics and crime problems in the local area, an analysis of official crime statistics using the FBI's Uniform Crime Reports, a summary of the findings, and recommendations based on the findings.

Both investigative and administrative reports may be formatted as memos and written to specific audiences who need the information to make decisions, formulate policy, and implement recommendations. In all cases, accuracy, completeness, and objectivity are key to an effective report.

Policy memos

Policy memos are written for many purposes—to inform, to explain, to document, to persuade, or to make a request. The format and style will vary from organization to organization, so you must be aware of the audience's expectations and the conventions set by the organization you're writing for. Typically, the purpose of a policy memo is to help the audience understand the issue and interpret the policy to make practical judgments. You might be asked to write a policy memo to the head of a criminal justice organization, such as the Transportation Security Administration, about the effects of racial profiling on a particular group. Your memo might include a description of the policies being used to address the problem; an argument, based on research, for changing the policies; and recommendations for policies or programs that would benefit the group about which you're concerned.

Case briefs and legal briefs

A brief is a document presented to interested members of a court of law. Briefs are addressed to a specific audience and typically include a short description of a legal case, highlighting key issues, relevant facts, and, if applicable, a history of related court decisions; an analysis and interpretation of how the case applies to a particular organization; and the legal principles and jurisdictional issues related to the desired outcome. For a case brief assignment, you might be asked to write to a public defender or a future judge on how to interpret issues involved in a specific case. A legal brief assignment might ask you to analyze documents submitted for a moot court exercise and to argue for one side.

Your instructor may ask you to follow the IRAC model when you write case and legal briefs. IRAC is an organizational approach used in legal writing as a method for problem solving and structuring an analysis. The acronym IRAC stands for the following steps:

Issue: State the legal issue of relevance.

Rules: List all the statutes and case law relevant to your brief.

Analysis or Application: Provide arguments in favor of and against the decision in this case.

Conclusion: Provide an answer to the legal issue raised.

Another organizational approach is based on the acronym PEAR:

Position: State a position.

Explanation: Explain the position.

Alternatives: Examine the alternative positions.

Response: Respond to potential objections.

NOTE: The explanations of the IRAC and PEAR models are adapted from the *Criminology, Law, and Society Writing Guide* from George Mason University at http://wac.gmu.edu/supporting/guides/CLS/.

Case plans (or case notes)

Case plans, or case notes, may be written as memos or as part of presentencing and postsentencing reports. They might be addressed to courtroom work groups, such as public defenders, prosecutors, judges, and probation officers. Case notes may be addressed to social workers and treatment providers in problem-solving courts such as drug and mental health courts. As the number of work groups expands, audience analysis becomes more complicated because each group may have different goals for its clients and constituencies. For example, a social worker might be interested in resources and treatment; lawyers, in justice; and judges, in the legal aspects of the case. Given the complexity of this writing task, there is no template to guide you. You will typically learn on the job or from models your instructor provides. In general, case notes and plans must be straightforward, clear, and well organized, with the goals and purpose carefully laid out in the introduction along with a preview of the main topics that you will cover. Be sure to include subheadings so that the various audiences can skim through the notes to identify information related to their concerns.

D4-c Know the questions criminal justice professionals and criminologists ask.

Generally, the questions that criminal justice professionals and criminologists ask can be divided into two broad areas of inquiry, one focused on legal systems, the other focused on justice organizations. Within these two broad areas are big-issue questions about crime, law enforcement, society, ethics, and social justice.

- What is deviance, and what is crime?
- What are the causes of crime?
- What is the difference between the law on the books and the law in action?
- What is effective policing?
- What are the theories and laws related to discretionary decision making for practitioners in the field?
- What policing, corrections, and court system policies and practices work to reduce crime and its social effects?

While most of your courses will take up these broad questions in one way or another, each course will have its own focusing questions. A course on policing in the United States, for example, will focus on the role of police in protecting the public against crime and disorder, influences on the decisions police make, the moral and ethical issues they confront, what good policing looks like, and the trends, innovations, and reforms that affect the policing profession. In a corrections course, the focus will be on postsentencing and postrelease issues, with questions about jail and prison management, probation and parole, and compliance with supervision and treatment follow-up requirements.

D4-d   Understand the kinds of evidence criminal justice professionals and criminologists use.

Criminal justice professionals and criminologists use many different kinds of evidence—quantitative, qualitative, historical, and legal—to answer the questions they pose. Most practitioners rely on methods derived from the social sciences to gather evidence: interviews, direct observation, surveys, narrative analysis, natural setting experiments, and analysis of demographic, statistical, legal, geographic, and historical data. Criminologists also use theory-based evidence or the history of a theory or law enforcement policy.

As a student, you will probably be required to use both primary and secondary sources as evidence and to gather and analyze both quantitative and qualitative data. Quantitative data may include crime statistics, incarceration rates, racial profiling data from police stops, ticketing rates, and data on crime statistics linked to geographic areas. Qualitative data may include your own observations, others' responses to interviews and surveys, and the stories people tell about their encounters with crime and the criminal justice system.

Your instructors will also expect you to consult relevant secondary sources, including articles in scholarly and popular periodicals (such as *Police Chief*), news media, government and legal documents, statistical reports, and organizational Web sites, reports, and studies.

D4-e   Become familiar with writing conventions in criminal justice and criminology.

Scholars and practitioners in the criminal justice field value independent thought; the ability to gather, synthesize, and analyze evidence from diverse sources; and the ability to interpret theory and to apply theory to practice and practice to theory. Beyond these broad goals, practitioners agree that writing in the field must be clear, concise, accurate, objective, and well organized, with a clear statement of the writer's purpose and main points. Writers must convey knowledge of the topic in a voice, tone, and format appropriate to the purpose and audience. They must present facts and evidence in an objective, balanced way to allow readers to draw their own conclusions.

To be objective, writers must strive for factual description. For example, in a crime report they should note the date, time, and location of a crime or suspected criminal behavior; they should also describe people and their actions as factually as possible, including identifying characteristics such as gender, race or ethnicity, age, height, weight, and distinctive features like facial hair, tattoos, scars, or physical mannerisms. Subjective descriptions such as "the perpetrator looked suspicious" are meaningless and unfair if not backed up with factual details. It is also important to avoid language that could be construed as offensive or that reveals biases toward gender, race, ethnicity, disabilities, and socioeconomic class.

In the criminal justice field, accuracy is crucial, whether in an arrest report, a briefing memo, a case plan, a researched report, or the application of a theory to an issue, a practice, or a policy. Errors and inaccuracies can cause readers to misinterpret a report, disregard a memo, or throw a case out of court.

First-person pronouns are rarely used in research papers, reports, policy memos, briefings, or analytical papers, in part because writers must present their views objectively, logically, and factually. While the writer of a memo or briefing report may use *I* on occasion, the content and the recommendations being made must be based on the writer's analysis of the evidence, not on personal opinions or biases. The diverse audiences for these documents also expect clear, concise writing, so writers typically use the active voice and paraphrases rather than extensive quotations from their research. In some circumstances, however, it is important to include direct quotations as this information might be critical to an accurate interpretation of the problem, issue, or policy.

D4-f Use the APA or CMS (*Chicago*) system in writing in criminal justice and criminology.

While professionals in the field generally use the documentation style prescribed by the organization or academic journal for which they are writing, instructors typically ask students to use the style guidelines of the American Psychological Association (APA) or the name-year system of *The Chicago Manual of Style* (CMS) to format their paper, to document sources in the text of their paper, and to list sources at the end. Both systems call for in-text, parenthetical citations rather than footnotes or endnotes. The APA system is set forth in the *Publication Manual of the American Psychological Association*, 6th ed. (Washington, DC: APA, 2010). CMS style is found in *The Chicago Manual of Style*, 16th ed. (Chicago: University of Chicago Press, 2010). (For more details, see the documentation sections in your handbook.)

Sometimes students are asked to use *Bluebook* style (or, as it's sometimes called, modified Bluebooking) when they cite sources in case briefs and legal briefs. *Bluebook* format is used by courts, attorneys, and law schools; however, most instructors do not require students to learn this specialized style.

D4-g Sample student paper: Administrative report

Administrative reports are written for specific audiences, typically supervisors, to provide information about an issue or a problem of concern to an organization. When you are asked to write a report, you will be expected to identify the issue or problem, find and analyze relevant statistics and other research, and make recommendations for future actions.

The following administrative report was written for an introductory course on crime and crime policy. Students were asked to imagine that they had been hired as a consultant by the new police chief in their hometown. They were asked to brief the chief about crime in the area, to explain how crime statistics for their town compare with the national average using the FBI's Uniform Crime Reports, and to interpret the statistics so that the chief could decide how best to use the department's resources. The student writer, Chris Thompson, analyzed crime statistics for his hometown of Leesburg, Virginia. He used APA guidelines to format his paper and to cite and list his sources.

Running head: CRIME IN LEESBURG, VIRGINIA   1

The header consists of a shortened title in all capital letters at the left margin and the page number at the right margin; on the title page only, the shortened title is preceded by the words "Running head" and a colon.

Crime in Leesburg, Virginia

Chris Thompson

George Mason University

Full title, writer's name, and school, halfway down the page.

An author's note lists specific information about the course or department and can provide acknowledgments and contact information.

Author Note

This paper was prepared for Administration of Justice 305: Crime Policy, taught by Professor Devon Johnson.

Marginal annotations indicate APA-style formatting and effective writing.

Full title, repeated.

Introduction
establishes
the purpose of
the report and
acknowledges the
audience.

Centered headings
define the major
sections of the
report.

Thompson provides
demographic
information
relevant to the
crime statistics he
will analyze.

In-text citation from
a Web site is in APA
style.

Thompson points
to the data tables,
explaining their
purpose and sources.

Thompson uses a
major section of the
report to analyze
details from the
tables.

Crime in Leesburg, Virginia

This report reviews crime statistics in Leesburg, Virginia, to familiarize the new police chief with the town and offer some suggestions about where to focus law enforcement resources. It analyzes local and national statistics from the FBI's Uniform Crime Reports (UCR) for the United States and for Leesburg and offers a basic assessment of the town's needs to provide a useful snapshot for the chief of police.

Description of Leesburg, Virginia

Leesburg, Virginia, is a suburb of Washington, DC, 40 miles to the northwest. In 2008, its population was 39,899 (U.S. Department of Justice, 2009, Table 8). Like many northern Virginia and southern Maryland communities, it serves as a suburban bedroom community to those employed in the nation's capital. The town has grown significantly in the last three decades.

Leesburg's population is predominantly middle and upper middle class, with a median household income 75% higher than the national average (Town of Leesburg, Virginia, 2009a). Leesburg is populated by young (median age 32.3), well-educated (about 50% with a bachelor's degree, about 17% with an advanced degree) citizens; half are white-collar professionals (Town of Leesburg, Virginia, 2009a).

The Leesburg Police Department has 77 sworn officers, operates 24 hours a day, and uses numerous special teams and modern law enforcement techniques. The department has divided the city into three patrol areas to address the specific needs of each zone (Town of Leesburg, Virginia, 2009b).

Nature and Extent of Crime in Leesburg, Virginia

Tables 1 and 2 show the FBI's UCR statistics for 2008. Table 1 contains statistics for Leesburg and the United States, and Table 2 presents the crime rate in Leesburg as a percentage of the national average. A discussion of the accuracy of the UCR is on page 5.

Crime Rates in Leesburg Compared With the National Average

The following list of index crimes compares their rates in Leesburg, Virginia (first value), with the national average (second value). In general, the crime rate in Leesburg is lower than it is across the country. This may be due in part to the demographics of the town's residents and the commuter-oriented suburban nature of the community.

CRIME IN LEESBURG, VIRGINIA   3

Table 1

Crime Rates, by Crime, in Leesburg, Virginia, and in the United States, 2008

	Leesburg		United States	
Offense type	No. reported offenses	Rate per 100,000 inhabitants	No. reported offenses	Rate per 100,000 inhabitants
Violent crime				
Forcible rape	7	17.5	89,000	29.3
Murder and nonnegligent manslaughter	1	2.5	16,272	5.4
Robbery	22	55.1	441,855	145.3
Aggravated assault	29	72.7	834,885	274.6
Total violent crime	59	147.8	1,382,012	454.5
Property crime				
Larceny theft	715	1,792	6,588,873	2,167
Burglary	62	155.4	2,222,196	730.8
Vehicle theft	25	62.7	956,846	314.7
Total property crime	802	2,010	9,767,915	3,212.5

Note. The data for Leesburg, Virginia, are from U.S. Department of Justice (2009), Table 8. The data for the United States are from U.S. Department of Justice (2009), Table 1.

Larceny Theft: 1,792 vs. 2,167 per 100,000

Larceny theft is one of the few index crimes found close to the same level in Leesburg as in the entire nation and thus represents an area of interest for the Leesburg police.

Forcible Rape: 17.5 vs. 29.3 per 100,000

The incidence of forcible rape is slightly more than half the national average. Rape crimes may be an area of concern in Leesburg.

Murder and Nonnegligent Manslaughter: 2.5 vs. 5.4 per 100,000

The most serious crimes, those involving the loss of a human life, are approximately half as prevalent in Leesburg as in the United States as a whole. Murder is typically not a crime that can be countered through patrol.

Robbery: 55.1 vs. 145.3 per 100,000

Robbery (a direct, personal theft from an individual) in Leesburg

---

The data tables are presented in APA style. The columns are clearly labeled, and the data categories reinforce the writer's purpose.

Thompson organizes his discussion of the crimes in Leesburg by most to least concerning.

Subheadings are flush left and boldface.

D4-g Writing in criminal justice and criminology

Table 2

*Crime Rates in Leesburg, Virginia, Compared With the National
Average, 2008*

Offense type	Crime rate in Leesburg per 100,000 inhabitants	Crime rate in the United States per 100,000 inhabitants	Crime rate in Leesburg compared with national average (%)
Violent crime			
Forcible rape	17.5	29.3	59.7
Murder and nonnegligent manslaughter	2.5	5.4	46.2
Robbery	55.1	145.3	37.9
Aggravated assault	72.7	274.6	26.4
Total violent crime	147.8	454.5	32.5
Property crime			
Larceny theft	1,792	2,167	82.6
Burglary	155.4	730.8	21.2
Vehicle theft	62.7	314.7	19.9
Total property crime	2,010	3,212.5	62.5

Note. The data for Leesburg, Virginia, are from U.S. Department of
Justice (2009), Table 8. The data for the United States are from U.S.
Department of Justice (2009), Table 1.

is approximately one-third the national average. Leesburg is not prone
to the frequency of robberies found in urban areas, perhaps because
most robberies are committed by residents of the same community,
and the community of Leesburg is fairly homogeneous in terms of
income levels.

Aggravated Assault: 72.7 vs. 274.6 per 100,000

The rate of felony assaults (attempts to commit or acts resulting in
serious bodily harm) in Leesburg is roughly one-quarter that in the nation
as a whole.

Burglary: 155.4 vs. 730.8 per 100,000

The incidence of burglary (breaking into the home of another
person with the intent to commit a felony) in Leesburg is one-fifth the
national average. The suburban nature of Leesburg may contribute to this
low level.

CRIME IN LEESBURG, VIRGINIA   5

Vehicle Theft: 62.7 vs. 314.7 per 100,000

Motor vehicle theft is uncommon in Leesburg, about one-fifth as likely as in the nation as a whole.

Areas of Interest for a New Police Chief

Overall, forcible rape and larceny theft are the two crimes of most interest to the Leesburg police because their frequency is closer to the national average than the frequency of other crimes. While overall crime is low in Leesburg, these two crimes stand out based solely on the FBI UCR statistics. The police may want to pay particular attention to these crimes for reasons not apparent in the UCR.

Forcible rape is typically an underreported crime because of victim-related factors such as shame and distrust of the system. This crime is of particular concern because even the UCR statistics may not reflect an accurate crime rate (Mosher, Miethe, & Phillips, 2002). The actual instances of rape may be significantly higher than those reported in the UCR. Policy implications may include an increased community policing focus on rape prevention as well as targeted police patrolling of areas where reported rapes occur.

The desire to file an insurance claim for larceny theft (which often requires a police report) may cause more citizens to come forward when they are victims of this particular crime. For this reason, the actual instances of larceny theft are likely closer to those captured in the UCR. Increased patrolling of residential neighborhoods during work hours may reduce burglary rates because most burglaries occur during the day when the occupants are at work.

Accuracy of UCR Statistics

The FBI's UCR, while useful in showing crime trends, is not without its faults. The UCR contains only crimes reported to or observed by law enforcement officers; therefore, it does not provide a complete portrait of crime. The National Crime Victimization Survey (NCVS) revealed that, in many cases, roughly half of the total crimes committed in the United States go unreported (Mosher et al., 2002). The reasons vary but include distrust or lack of faith in the police and the judicial system, shame about or apathy toward the crime, fear of reprisals, inability to recognize the perpetrator, and victim participation in illegal activities at the time of

Thompson interprets the crime statistics and makes recommendations for allocating department resources.

Thompson discusses issues related to the reporting of crime and the accuracy of the UCR. To analyze the strengths and weaknesses of the UCR, he draws on secondary sources.

CRIME IN LEESBURG, VIRGINIA   6

In APA style for a work with three to five authors, all authors are given the first time the source is cited; in subsequent citations, the first author is followed by "et al."

victimization (Mosher et al., 2002). The new police chief should keep these limitations in mind when evaluating UCR statistics.

In addition, classifying crimes is often subjective. Mosher et al. (2002) pointed out that "political manipulation and fabrication of these data by police departments" can easily distort statistics related to an individual incident or a whole reporting agency (p. 84). Some of these distortions are a product of police officer discretion stemming from the "legal seriousness of the crime," "the complainant's preferences," any relationship between the police officer and the offender, the level of respect shown by the complainant, and the financial or social status of the complainant (p. 85).

Conclusion

Thompson summarizes the findings in the report and provides a recommendation. He ends by explaining the importance of crime data analysis for policymaking and assessment.

The town of Leesburg, Virginia, is, in general, a safe place to live. Overall, it experiences a rate of crime considerably lower than the national average. The incidence of property crime is 62.5% of the national average, and the incidence of violent crime is 32.5% of the national average. Leesburg does, however, have two potential problem areas: forcible rape and larceny theft.

This report's initial examination of the data from the UCR is of limited value because of the UCR's lack of depth and breadth in exploring local crime. To obtain a better picture of crime in Leesburg, the new police chief should request a report that compares local, regional, and national crime statistics over several years using the FBI's UCR combined with NCVS data to develop an accurate picture of overall crime. Carefully weighing that information and evaluating it to reveal the big picture are both a means and an end in the law enforcement world: They allow policymakers to make decisions that may reduce the crime rate.

CRIME IN LEESBURG, VIRGINIA 7

References

Mosher, C. J., Miethe, T. D., & Phillips, D. M. (2002). *The mismeasure of crime*. Thousand Oaks, CA: Sage.

Town of Leesburg, Virginia. (2009a). *Demographics*. Retrieved from http://www.leesburgva.gov/index.aspx?page=210

Town of Leesburg, Virginia. (2009b). *Field operations division*. Retrieved from http://www.leesburgva.gov/index.aspx?page=955

U.S. Department of Justice, Federal Bureau of Investigation. (2009). *Crime in the United States 2008*. Retrieved from http://www2.fbi.gov/ucr/cius2008/index.html

List of references is in APA style.

List of references begins on a new page. The first line of each entry is at the left margin; subsequent lines indent ½".

D5   Writing in education

The field of education draws on the knowledge and the methods of a variety of disciplines. As you study to become a teacher, you will take courses that focus on such diverse topics as the history of education, the psychology of teaching and learning, the development of curriculum, and instructional methods. You will also learn how to navigate classrooms and schools through both course work and field placements. Depending on what you plan to teach, you may also take courses in a specific content area (such as history or mathematics) or courses that focus on children with special needs. The writing you do in education courses will be designed to help you become a successful teacher.

D5-a Determine your audience and their needs in education.

Audiences in the field of education may be school administrators, teachers, students, parents, or policymakers. Administrators read documents to evaluate faculty and assess programs, to revise or develop new programs and curricula, to create policy, to solve problems, to resolve student issues, and to communicate with parents. Teachers read scholarship in their fields to learn about new theoretical findings and methods. Because assessment is a major topic in academic institutions, teachers read reports on student and program assessment as well as informational documents that help them participate in making school policy for testing and placement. Students and parents read publications from their schools and school districts to learn about student performance and school policy. Policymakers such as school board members and state legislators expect information, assessment reports, and proposals about schools, curricula, and programs to be presented with numerical data in the form of graphs and tables.

When you write in education courses, be sure to give your readers empirical data, such as test scores, presented in an easily understandable format. You may need to provide direct observations of student performance as well. Always maintain student confidentiality. Because student groups are so diverse and because positive community relations are essential to every school, be sensitive to student backgrounds and respectful toward students and parents.

D5-b   Recognize the forms of writing in education.

Although there are many paths you can take as you train to become a teacher, you will encounter similar writing assignments in different courses. These may include the following:

- reflective essays, journals, and field notes
- curriculum designs and lesson plans
- reviews of instructional materials
- case studies
- research papers
- self-evaluations
- portfolios

Reflective essays, journals, and field notes

Much of the writing you do in education courses will encourage you to reflect on your own attitudes, beliefs, and experiences and how they inform your thoughts about teaching and learning. In an introductory course, for example, you may be asked to write an essay in which you discuss your own education in the context of a theory that you are studying. As a field observer or student teacher, you may be asked to keep a journal or notes in which you reflect on teacher-student interactions, student-student interactions, diversity issues, and student progress. These reflections might then serve as the basis for an essay in which you connect your experiences to course content.

Curriculum designs and lesson plans

In some courses, especially those focused on teaching methods, you will be asked to design individual lessons or units in a particular content area. In an early childhood education course, for example, you might be asked to read one or more children's books and write a plan for a class activity that is related to the reading. In a science methods course, you might be asked to design a unit about plant biology. In a methods course for special education, you might be asked to design an individualized education plan for a specific student. For any of these courses, you might also be asked to integrate technology into your curriculum design.

Reviews of instructional materials

In a review of materials, you assess the value of a set of instructional materials for classroom use. For example, you might be asked to look at several textbooks or software applications and explain which would be most useful in a particular classroom setting.

Case studies

Some education courses require students to conduct and write case studies. Case studies may involve observation and analysis of an individual student, a teacher, or classroom interactions. The goal of a case study may be to determine how the process of teaching or learning takes place or how an event can illuminate something about learning or classroom dynamics.

Research papers

In some education courses, you might be assigned papers that focus on broader educational issues or problems and that require you to conduct research and then formulate your own ideas about the topic. In a course about the history of education, you might be asked to research the evolution of literacy in the United States. In a developmental psychology course, you might be asked to research how students learn mathematics.

Self-evaluations

As a teacher candidate, you will be asked to evaluate your own teaching and learning. The format of the self-evaluation will vary depending on whether you are evaluating yourself as a learner or as a teacher. Sample questions of self-evaluation as a teacher may include the following:

- What were the strengths and weaknesses of your lesson or unit plan?
- How did your lesson further student learning?
- What have you learned about yourself and your students from teaching this class?
- How can you improve your teaching?

Portfolios

Most teacher education programs require you to assemble a teaching portfolio before you graduate. The purpose of the portfolio is to provide information about your teaching experience and your teaching philosophy. The contents of portfolios vary, but common documents include a statement of teaching philosophy, a statement of professional goals, a résumé, evaluations, and sample course materials. Education departments at some institutions will require you to assemble an electronic portfolio as well as a print version.

D5-c Know the questions educators ask.

Educators ask questions that are practical, theoretical, and self-reflective. Practical questions tend to focus on classroom and curriculum issues such as student progress and implementation of new approaches. Theoretical questions focus on how students should be educated and on the intellectual, political, and social contexts of learning. Self-reflective questions allow for discussion of the teacher's own role in the educational process. Any of the following questions could form the basis for a paper in an education course.

- How does this school's language arts curriculum prepare students to be information-literate?
- What are the effects of the use of standardized tests in economically disadvantaged districts in comparison with more affluent districts?
- How do my perceptions of my own education influence the way I approach teaching?

D5-d Understand the kinds of evidence educators use.

Educators and education students rely on evidence that is both quantitative (statistics, survey results, test scores) and qualitative (case studies, observation, personal experience). The following are some examples of evidence used in different situations.

- If you are writing a research paper that compares different approaches to social studies education, you might rely on quantitative evidence such as the results of standardized tests from different school districts.
- For a paper on child development, you might use a combination of personal observation and evidence from published case studies.
- If you are keeping a journal of your student teaching experiences, your evidence would come from your experiences in the classroom and from the changes in your attitudes over time.
- If you are creating a lesson plan, you will focus on your teaching objectives and explain how your plan will achieve those objectives.

D5-e Become familiar with writing conventions in education.

Educators agree on several conventions when they write.

- The personal pronoun *I* is commonly used in reflective writing. It is sometimes used to communicate observations and recommendations.

- Research papers and case studies are generally written in the third person (*he, she, it, they*) and in a formal, objective tone.

- Educators have a specialized vocabulary that includes terms such as *pedagogy* (teaching principles and methods), *practice* (actual teaching), *curriculum* (the written lesson plans followed by a class or school), *assessment* (the determination of whether students or teachers are successful), *achievement tests* (tests that measure what students have learned), and *NCLB* (the No Child Left Behind Act). You will likely use such terms in your writing.

Because the field of education draws on various disciplines, including psychology, history, and sociology, it is important to be aware of writing conventions in those disciplines as well. (See D7 and D10.)

D5-f Use the APA or CMS (*Chicago*) system in writing in education.

Writers in education typically use the style guidelines of the American Psychological Association (APA) or *The Chicago Manual of Style* (CMS) for formatting their paper, for citing sources in the text of their paper, and for listing sources at the end. The APA system is set forth in the *Publication Manual of the American Psychological Association*, 6th ed. (Washington, DC: APA, 2010). CMS style is found in *The Chicago Manual of Style*, 16th ed. (Chicago: University of Chicago Press, 2010). (For more details, see the documentation sections in your handbook.) In education courses, instructors will usually indicate which style they prefer.

D5-g Sample student paper: Reflective essay

In some education courses, you may be asked to write reflective essays in which you describe and analyze your own attitudes, beliefs, and experiences. Some reflective essays focus solely on personal observations while others integrate ideas from other sources as well.

The following reflective essay was written for a service learning course in which students explored issues of diversity, power, and opportunity in school settings. The writer, Onnalee Gibson, used a variety of professional sources to inform her own ideas about her experiences working with an eleventh-grade student. She formatted her paper and cited and listed her sources following the guidelines of the American Psychological Association (APA).

The header consists of a shortened title in all capital letters at the left margin and the page number at the right margin; on the title page only, the shortened title is preceded by the words "Running head" and a colon.

A Reflection on Service Learning:

Working with Eric

Onnalee L. Gibson

Michigan State University

Full title, writer's name, and school halfway down the page.

An author's note lists specific information about the course or department and can provide acknowledgments and contact information.

Author Note

This paper was prepared for Teacher Education 250, taught by Professor Carter. The author wishes to thank the guidance staff of Waverly High School for advice and assistance.

Marginal annotations indicate APA-style formatting and effective writing.

SERVICE LEARNING: ERIC   2

A Reflection on Service Learning:

Working with Eric

The first time I saw the beautiful yet simple architecture of Waverly High School, I was enchanted. I remember driving by while exploring my new surroundings as a transfer student to Michigan State University and marveling at the long front wall of reflective windows, the shapely bushes, and the general cleanliness of the school grounds. When I was assigned to do a service learning project in a local school district, I hoped for the opportunity to find out what it would be like to work at a school like Waverly—a school where the attention to its students' needs was evident from the outside in.

> Reflective essays may include descriptive passages.

Waverly High School, which currently enrolls about 1,100 students in grades 9 through 12 and has a teaching staff of 63, is extremely diverse in several ways. Economically, students range from poverty level to affluent. Numerous ethnic and racial groups are represented. And in terms of achievement, the student body boasts an assortment of talents and abilities.

> Background information about the school sets the scene for Gibson's personal experiences.

The school provides a curriculum that strives to meet the needs of each student and uses a unique grade reporting system that itemizes each aspect of a student's grade. The system allows both teachers and parents to see where academic achievement and academic problems surface. Unlike most schools, which evaluate students on subjects in one number or letter grade, Waverly has a report card that lists individual grades for tests, homework, exams, papers, projects, participation, community service, and attendance. Thus, if a student is doing every homework assignment and is still failing tests, this breakdown of the grades may effectively highlight how the student can be helped.

It was this unique way of evaluating students that led to my first meeting with Eric Johnson, an 11th grader to whom I was assigned as a tutor. Eric is an African American male who grew up in a nuclear middle-class family in a Lansing suburb. Teachers noticed over time that Eric's grades were dropping, yet his attendance, participation, and motivation were above average. Surprisingly, Eric himself was the one who asked for a tutor to help him raise his grades. What initially struck me about Eric was the level of responsibility he seemed to take for his own academic

> Transition leads from background information about the school to Gibson's personal experiences.

SERVICE LEARNING: ERIC   3

Journal entries are
considered personal
communication and
are cited in the text
but not included in
the reference list.

achievement. At the time I wrote in my journal (January 31, 2006), "He
appears to be a good student. He is trying his best to succeed in school.
He came to *me* for help and realizes the need for a tutor."

While tutoring Eric, I paid attention to the way he talked about his
classes and to the types of assignments he was being asked to complete.
My impression was that Waverly High School was fostering student

Personal
observations lead
to broader insights.

success by doing more than just placing posters in the hallways. Waverly's
curriculum encourages analytical thinking, requires group and individual
projects that depend on creativity and research, and includes open-ended
writing assignments designed to give students opportunities to form their
own conclusions. I found this reality both difficult and inspiring; I had not
expected an 11th grader's homework to be so challenging. I once said so
to Eric, and he responded with a smile: "Yeah. My teachers say it's going to
help us when we get to college to already know how to do some of these
things."

What was surprising to me was the faculty's collective assumption
that high school was not the end of a student's career. The fact that
teachers talk with students about what will be expected *when* (not *if*) they

Gibson analyzes her
evidence to draw a
broader conclusion.

go to college is significant. That kind of positive language, which I heard
many times at Waverly, most certainly affects students' sense of themselves
as achievers. In this case, Eric was not preoccupied with worrying about
whether he wanted to go to college or would be accepted; rather, he
mentally prepared himself for the time when he would actually enroll.

This section bridges
academic theory
and personal
experience.

According to education researcher Jean Anyon (1981), "Students
from higher social class backgrounds may be exposed to legal, medical,
or managerial knowledge . . . while those of the working classes may be
offered a more 'practical' curriculum" (p. 5). I do not see this gravitation
toward social reproduction holding true for most students at Waverly High
School. Waverly's student body is a mix of social classes, yet the school's
philosophy is to push each of its students to consider college. Through its
curriculum, its guidance department literature, and its opportunities for
career field trips, Waverly is opening doors for all of its students. In Eric's
case, I also observed the beginnings of a break in social reproduction. From
the start of our tutoring sessions, Eric frequently mentioned that neither of
his parents went to college (O. Gibson, journal entry, March 14, 2006). This

SERVICE LEARNING: ERIC   4

made me wonder how his parents talk to him about college. Is the desire to go to college something they have instilled in him? Have they given him the message that if he works hard and goes to college he will be successful? If that is the case, then Eric's parents are attempting to break the cycle with their children—and they have the good fortune to live in a school district that supports their desires. In contrast to the idea that most people have nothing more than social reproduction to thank for their socioeconomic status (Bowles & Gintis, 1976), Eric seems to believe that hard work and a college education are keys to his success.

> Source is cited in APA in-text citation style.

Another key to Eric's success will be the resources he enjoys as a student at Waverly. Abundance of or lack of resources can play an important part in students' opportunities to learn and succeed. Because nearly half of all school funding comes from local property taxes (D. Carter, class lecture, April 4, 2006), areas with smaller populations or low property values do not have the tax base to fund schools well. As a result, one education finance expert has argued, some children receive substandard education (Parrish, 2002). Waverly does not appear to have serious financial or funding issues. Each student has access to current textbooks, up-to-date computer labs, a well-stocked library, a full art and music curriculum, and numerous extracurricular activities. While countless schools are in desperate need of a better-equipped library, Waverly's library has a rich collection of books, magazines and journals, computer stations, and spaces in which to use all of these materials. It is a very user-friendly library. This has shown me what the power of funding can do for a school. Part of Waverly's (and its students') success results from the ample resources spent on staff and curriculum materials. Adequate school funding is one of the factors that drive school and student success.

> Class lecture (personal communication) is cited in the text only, not in the reference list.

> Gibson considers the larger implications of her personal observations.

Aside from funding, placement policies determine school and student success. A major concern of both educators and critics of education policies is that schools will place students into special education programs unnecessarily. Too often students who do not need special education are coded for special ed—even when they have a learning issue that can be handled with a good teacher in a mainstream class (D. Carter, class lecture, April 6, 2006). At Waverly High School, teachers and counselors are not so quick to shuffle Eric into special ed. I agree with several of Eric's teachers

SERVICE LEARNING: ERIC   5

who feel that he may have a mild learning disability. I began to feel this
way when Eric and I moved from working in a private tutoring space to
working in the library. It was clear to me that he had difficulty paying
attention in a public setting. On February 9, I wrote in my journal:

A quotation longer
than forty words is
indented without
quotation marks.

> Eric was extremely distracted. He couldn't pay attention to what I
> was asking, and he couldn't keep his eyes on his work. There were
> other students in the library today, and he kept eavesdropping on
> their conversations and shaking his head when they said things he
> did not agree with. This is how he must behave in the classroom; he
> is easily distracted but he wants to work hard. I see that it is not
> so much that he needs a tutor because he can't understand what his
> teachers are telling him; it is more that he needs the one-on-one
> attention in a confined room free of distractions.

Even though Eric showed signs of distraction, I never felt as
if he should be coded for special education. I am pleased that the
administration and learning specialists did not decide to place Eric in a
special education track. Eric is exceedingly intelligent and shows promise
in every academic area. He seems to be able to succeed by identifying
problems on his own and seeking resources to help him solve those
problems. He is a motivated and talented student who simply seems like
a typical adolescent.

I came away from my service learning project with an even stronger
conviction about the importance of quality education for a student's
success. Unlike the high school I attended, Waverly pays close attention
to each child and thinks about how to get all its students to succeed
at their own level. Jean Patrice, an administrator, told me, "You have
to be able to reach a student where *they* are instead of making them
come to you. If you don't, you'll lose them" (personal communication,
April 10, 2006), expressing her desire to see all students get something
out of their educational experience. This feeling is common among
members of Waverly's faculty. With such a positive view of student
potential, it is no wonder that 97% of Waverly High School graduates go
on to a four-year university (Patrice, 2006). I have no doubt that Eric
Johnson will attend college and that he will succeed there.

As I look toward my teaching future, I know there is plenty that I

SERVICE LEARNING: ERIC   6

have left to learn. Teaching is so much more than getting up in front of a
class, reiterating facts, and requiring students to learn a certain amount of
material by the end of the year. Teaching is about getting students—one
by one—to realize and act on their potential. This course and this service
learning experience have made me realize that we should never have a
trial-and-error attitude about any student's opportunities and educational
quality.

Conclusion raises
questions for
further reflection.

SERVICE LEARNING: ERIC   7

List of references,
in APA style, begins
on a new page.

List is alphabetized
by authors' last
names.

Double-spacing is
used throughout.

                              References

Anyon, J. (1981). Social class and school knowledge. *Curriculum Inquiry*,
        11(1), 5.

Bowles, S., & Gintis, H. (1976). *Schooling in capitalist America: Educational
        reform and contradictions of economic life.* New York, NY: Basic
        Books.

Parrish, T. (2002). Racial disparities in identification, funding, and
        provision of special education. In D. Losen & G. Orfield (Eds.), *Racial
        inequity in special education.* Cambridge, MA: Civil Rights Project and
        Harvard Education Press.

D6 Writing in engineering

Engineers use the language of mathematics and the methods of science along with the experiences of society to design machines, tools, processes, and systems that will solve problems and accomplish tasks safely and efficiently. There are many different types of engineers: mechanical, chemical, electrical, civil, geological, environmental, and aerospace, to name a few. Each type of engineer addresses problems and tasks in a particular part of the physical world.

Writing plays a major role in the work of engineers, who write reports and recommendations based on their research and their design ideas. Engineers write technical reports addressed to manufacturers or the companies or agencies that hire them. Engineers also communicate their solutions to clients in their own organizations.

As a student of engineering, you will be challenged to devise solutions to real-world problems. Most of your assignments will be open-ended questions that will involve finding or proposing solutions to design challenges; you will be required to compose rationales for your solutions in writing. In laboratory experiments, you will maintain a lab notebook and write reports about your hands-on research. Because engineers usually work in teams, some writing assignments will involve working with other students to give you practice with collaboration.

D6-a Determine your audience and their needs in engineering.

Engineers usually write for readers who have a definite interest in what they have to say. Research and design in engineering never take place in isolation; these activities occur in universities, private industry, and government.

Sometimes your readers will be other engineers and decision makers working in your team or in other groups in your organization; they will expect you to provide a high level of technical detail and to use specialized vocabulary. They need to be able to replicate your work and confirm the results. Sometimes your audience will be a corporate client outside your organization in industry or government. Or your audience might be public-policy decision makers or the general public. Some of these audiences might not have your level of technical expertise, so your writing must be accessible and clear, with a minimum of technical language and jargon. For example, if you are writing a proposal to win a contract for your company or to receive funding for a project, your proposal will have to be written appropriately for an audience consisting of both specialists and nonspecialists.

When you write in engineering courses, keep in mind that you are learning to write for readers who probably have not done the study, research, or design work that you have done. When writing a report, for example, you will write for a reader who was not present in the laboratory or in the field. Even though your professor is in the laboratory with you, always describe your research and experimentation process carefully and thoroughly as if he or she is not familiar with your process. Add spreadsheets, drawings, plates, or illustrations to help your readers visualize your findings.

D6-b   Recognize the forms of writing in engineering.

When you take courses in engineering, you may be asked to write any of the following:

- project notebooks
- laboratory reports
- technical reports
- proposals
- progress reports

Project notebooks

A project notebook is like a personal journal in which you record your work in progress. It is a log in which you can write your observations and data from the experimentation and design processes or brainstorm and explore explanations or interpretations of the data. You might describe the materials you use and the procedures you follow or draw sketches of your design and, later, its construction. A project notebook can be useful as you work through mathematical analysis of your data and your designs and as you pose questions and plan solutions to problems. It can also provide the space in which you make note of tests that work and those that do not. You can write reflections on articles you read, notes from meetings you attend, and logistics for projects you are working on. You might also record your instructor's and peers' comments and critiques.

Make your project notebook as complete and as neat as possible; sign and date entries daily. Remember that your notebook will be useful in your later research, design, and writing. If your notebook is part of an ongoing project that someone else will continue after you, then formality, thoroughness, and neatness will be critical. Notebooks are traditionally kept on paper, but you may keep one electronically to make it easier to record, update, and read. As you move into professional practice, these notebooks will become part of any project's formal records.

Laboratory reports

Engineers present the procedures, materials, and results of their experiments in laboratory reports. These reports are essential to the development of the discipline, as it is through these reports that new knowledge is recorded and communicated to researchers, teachers, and students. Laboratory reports for some assignments may have particular requirements. Generally, the laboratory reports you are assigned will follow the organization used in laboratory reports written by engineers working in industry and government.

Your report will need to accomplish the following:

- establish the main question or problem under investigation and provide some background
- state the objective of the laboratory work (to measure, to verify, to compare, and so on) and the exact methods and procedures step-by-step
- describe and comment on your results, explain what they mean, put any unexpected results in context, and compare your results with established knowledge in the discipline
- place your results in the context of your stated purpose; note patterns apparent in the results, implications for future consideration, and any questions that remain unanswered
- tell your reader if you achieved the predicted or anticipated results; account for any differences if possible

The structure of your laboratory report will function as "instructions" for anyone who wants to replicate your experiment, verify your results, or use your work as a foundation for his or her own research.

You can use the same method and structure to record and report on engineering design projects.

Technical reports

A technical report describes the structure and functions of a design. If the report's purpose is to investigate the failure of a design, tool, or machine, then it is a *forensic report*. The audience for a technical or design report is usually other engineers or a similar audience of experts; it can also be decision makers, regulators, and the courts.

A technical report usually has the following structure:

- executive summary, a one-page concise statement of the most important points in the report
- introduction
- purpose and goals
- methods
- data and findings
- recommendations and action items
- conclusion
- appendices if necessary

Use tables, charts, spreadsheets, maps, figures, and illustrations in the body of your report to present your data and findings or in appendices to support your conclusions. Your recommendations and conclusion should interpret your data, discuss any limitations or boundaries of your work, and suggest action items for this project or other, related projects. Document your work by citing your references in the style recommended by your instructor or the organization for which you are writing.

Proposals

Engineers write project proposals to seek funding from academic and government sources or to describe a project to potential clients. "Selling" a customer on a project is thus an important function of an engineer's job. Many proposals are written with cross-disciplinary teams including sales, marketing, production, and legal departments. A proposal for a client may include a price quote or estimate, also called a "bid."

For your classes, you may write proposals for laboratory projects or to suggest solutions for a hypothetical client (usually your professor) who has given you a technical problem or design problem. Prepare your proposals with sufficient research, appropriate graphics, careful organization, and neat presentation to assist your readers and show them that you are credible.

To make it easy for your readers to say yes to your proposal, give them clear, sufficient information about the project. Begin with an introduction that includes a brief project description and lays out the cost, completion date, and rate of return on investment. In the body of the proposal, provide the following:

- background and rationale for the project, describing the need to be met or the problem to be solved
- how the project will be accomplished
- expected outcomes

- materials and methods
- method of evaluation that will be used to determine that the objectives have been achieved
- timeline (sometimes presented in a Gantt chart, a graphical representation of the overlapping deadlines and milestones for all aspects of the project)
- budget, including deadlines and a list of items that must be funded

You can assume that your readers are receiving other proposals, so you might also provide a résumé or a section describing your skills and experiences that qualify you for the project.

Progress reports

Once a proposal is accepted and a project is under way, an engineer must write progress reports regularly to inform the client of the work accomplished. A progress report can be in the form of a business letter or a memo. It describes any milestones that have been achieved or tasks that have been completed. In engineering classes, your progress reports will be written to your professor to document your accomplishments and to describe the work still to be completed.

In your progress report, you might provide the following:

- a brief project description as a reminder of the scope of the project
- a summary of progress with a list of the tasks that have been completed
- a list of any problems that have arisen and solutions implemented or suggested
- any necessary alterations in deadlines or the budget
- a description of work remaining before the next progress report

Engineers frequently use spreadsheets to present data and provide a "snapshot" of the project at various stages. Spreadsheets can be converted into slides for PowerPoint presentations along with images of the work. Complete project reports will assure your readers that you are reliable, punctual, and in control of progress.

D6-c Know the questions engineers ask.

Engineers explore questions related to designing, repairing, and improving aspects of the physical world. Wherever people require a safer, faster, more effective, more efficient, more comfortable, or less expensive way to accomplish a task, engineers investigate and suggest solutions. The tasks might be related to transportation, to the construction of buildings and bridges, to the design of electrical grids and other city infrastructure, or to the invention of appliances and tools in the home or in the workplace.

Engineers explore questions such as these:

- An aging bridge in an area with heavy traffic must be replaced as soon as possible. What is the best design for a new bridge that can support a heavy payload but can also be built in a short period of time?

- Can a liquid laundry detergent be invented that will dissolve more quickly in water and flow more efficiently through the hoses of a new high-efficiency washing machine?

- What material would be best for resurfacing a parking lot in an area that often floods when it rains? What are the properties of different materials that might be used for this construction project?

- Two aerospace companies have proposed different configurations for the wings of a new fighter plane. Which of the two wing designs will allow the aircraft to achieve the highest possible speed with the lowest possible vibration at the most affordable cost?

- Is it possible to invent electronic devices that can be powered wirelessly rather than with batteries or electrical power?

- Understanding that customers want more environmentally friendly equipment for the home, a manufacturer of lawn mowers asks, Is it possible to construct a new kind of engine, similar to the engines in hybrid cars, that would burn fuel more efficiently and more cleanly than current engines?

D6-d Understand the kinds of evidence engineers use.

Engineers use particular kinds of evidence:

- data from laboratory reports published by other engineers
- observations and measurements of apparatus and processes inside the laboratory
- observations and measurements from building models of proposed projects
- observations and measurements from computer simulations and models
- observations and measurements made in real-world settings

Engineers often begin the design process with computer simulations and analysis. Then they verify the simulated results with models and laboratory experiments. This process saves money for engineering firms and their clients. For example, car companies use multiple computer simulations of car crashes before they crash-test a real car. In your classes, your projects may be "pen and paper" designs: You design and test the project on the computer or with manual calculations but do not actually build the project.

Data in engineering are quantitative; they can be counted. Depending on the nature of the problem or experiment, some data can be qualitative, described without numbers. When a structure fails or displays flaws, forensic engineers perform physical tests and sometimes collect and analyze witness testimony as they seek the causes of the problem.

For example, after a passenger airplane exploded in midair in 1996, engineers spent months reconstructing the aircraft to locate the cause. They discovered that structural problems had resulted in small vibrations. Over a long period of time, the vibrations had caused two electrical wires located near a fuel tank to rub against each other. Eventually the insulation of one of the wires had rubbed away, and the electrical current in the wire caused a spark that ignited vapors from the fuel tank. The engineers arrived at this conclusion only after painstakingly examining numerous components, sometimes in microscopic detail, ruling out many of them, focusing on the relevant ones, and ultimately performing tests in the laboratory to replicate the effects of vibrations on the wires.

D6-e Become familiar with writing conventions in engineering.

Engineers agree on several conventions when they write.

- Engineers often work in teams on research and laboratory projects. In your classes, you will often collaborate with other students. Collaboration requires that team members delegate and accept responsibility, report to one another, share ideas, listen to one another, negotiate differences, and compromise on solutions. Usually one person on the team will be in charge of combining the individually written sections of a report into a single document. Some team members may not be engineers or engineering students. Developing relationships with nonengineering and nonscience students and professionals is essential to effective work and communication in engineering.

- Each type of writing should include standard sections. For example, a laboratory report is not complete if it does not include a section that interprets results.

- Engineers must be brief and clear. When describing a process or an apparatus you used, you will need to write exactly what you did and what resulted. You must present the order of the steps you followed in logical sequence.

- Engineers try to avoid ambiguous pronoun use so that readers will know exactly what a pronoun refers to. Instead of writing *This confirms the original results*, an engineer should write *This new set of data confirms the original results*.

- Engineers use headings and subheadings in their reports and proposals. Engineering reports can be long and detailed, and headings mark the important categories of information and help readers follow the organization. Engineers also divide their reports into clear parts with combinations of numbers and letters denoting major sections and their subsections.

- Engineering is a visual field. Readers expect writers to provide diagrams, illustrations, charts, tables, and graphs. Graphics should support the data and other information in a report; they should be easy to understand, with clear labels and captions.

- Engineers use verb tenses deliberately. They use past tense for laboratory reports (*These results demonstrated*). They use future tense in proposals (*This design will require*). They use both present tense and past tense in progress reports (*The design phase is on schedule* or *The foundation was poured during week 3*).

- Engineers usually use third-person pronouns (*he, she, it, they* rather than *I, me, we*). They use the active voice where possible because it is more direct and concise. For instance, instead of writing *The viability of the instrument was demonstrated by the results*, they write *The results demonstrated the viability of the instrument*.

D6-f Use the CMS (*Chicago*), IEEE, or USGS system in writing in engineering.

Writers in different fields of engineering use different styles to cite sources in their papers and to list sources at the ends of their papers. Civil engineers, chemical engineers, industrial engineers, and mechanical engineers usually use the name-year system of *The Chicago Manual of Style*, 16th ed. (Chicago: University of Chicago Press, 2010).

Electrical engineers, computer engineers, and mechanical engineers use the *IEEE Citation Reference* (2009), published by the Institute of Electrical and Electronics Engineers.

Engineers and scientists in geology usually use *Suggestions to Authors of the Reports of the United States Geological Survey*, 7th ed. (Washington: GPO, 1991).

When you begin a project in an engineering class, check with your instructor about which style is required for your assignment.

D6-g Sample student paper: Proposal

A proposal recommends a solution to a design or technical problem posed by a client. A typical proposal includes details about how the project will be completed, the required materials and methods of construction, and the expected costs. It often includes alternatives for comparison. The following proposal was written in a junior-level geology engineering course. The student, Alice O'Bryan, explores the options that a fictional company called Ajax might consider for providing proper drainage for a planned park. O'Bryan presents descriptions of several alternatives, including costs, benefits, and overall effectiveness. She used the United States Geological Survey (USGS) guidelines to format her paper and to cite and list her sources.

O'Bryan 1

Full title, writer's name, course, and date, centered halfway down the page.

Site Stabilization Plan for Erosion Control

Alice O'Bryan

GLY 341

May 5, XXXX

Marginal annotations indicate USGS-style formatting and effective writing.

O'Bryan 2

CONTENTS

The contents page lists all the major headings and subheadings; it can also list minor subheadings, as shown here. The indentation of headings in the contents indicates the hierarchy and organization of the paper.

O'Bryan 3

A USGS proposal
often begins
with an executive
summary that
briefly provides
background,
findings, and
recommendations.

EXECUTIVE SUMMARY

Ajax is seeking to develop a 44-acre parcel of land into a recreational park and has requested proposals for erosion control. This proposal recommends a system of terraces and a grassed waterway culminating in a 1-acre constructed lake. While this is not the least expensive method of erosion control, it will be effective at preventing erosion and also will meet Ajax's goals for an aesthetically pleasing park that can attract human visitors as well as aquatic life and wildlife. Two less desirable plans are a system of terraces with a riprapped waterway and a buried pipeline. Both plans are less expensive, but both have drawbacks and do not meet all of Ajax's goals.

The recommended proposal (proposal A) will create a series of 13 vegetative terraces that flow into a grassed waterway approximately 1,200 feet long. The waterway will culminate in a 1-acre lake that will collect the drainage and provide a recreational fishing hole. This proposal has the advantage of not disrupting the open land and in fact enhancing it with planted vegetation along the terraces and waterway and with a lake that can attract wildlife and that can be used for recreational purposes. The cost of this proposal is as follows:

- Terraces: $15,034
- Grassed waterway: $4,000
- 1-acre lake: $18,000-60,000
- Total: $37,034-79,034

Additional costs will be incurred for recovery of the soil if more surface is disturbed than just the terrace and waterway construction areas. (See the summary of costs at the end of the proposal.)

The proposal for terraces and a riprapped waterway (proposal B) includes a riprapped channel that would disrupt the parklike atmosphere and that may not prevent off-site erosion. Its costs are as follows:

- Terraces: $15,034
- Riprapped waterway: $6,000
- Total: $21,034

The buried pipeline (proposal C) is the least desirable option because it is hard to maintain, requires an unattractive retaining wall, and is not suited for the soil type in this area. Its costs are as follows:

O'Bryan 4

- Buried pipeline: $6,000
- Gabion retaining wall: $25,000-50,000
- Total: $31,000-56,000

ANALYSIS OF PROPOSALS

PROPOSAL A: TERRACES AND GRASSED WATERWAY

Nonstructural and preventive erosion control provided by proposal A is the best choice for Ajax because the land is to be developed into a park. It is not the least expensive method, but it is likely to be most effective at meeting all the goals of the project. This proposal recommends a system of 7 terraces, each pair spaced 120 feet apart in the clayey silt soil, and 6 terraces, each pair spaced 150 feet apart in the silty clay soil. These terraces would have a 0.60% channel gradient, which would direct the water into a grassed waterway culminating in a 1-acre lake. A lake of this size is reasonable on a site of 44 acres and is more cost-effective than a smaller lake or a pond, which requires more specialized equipment to construct. The site is well suited for a lake because of its gently sloping topography. While a well-built lake can be expensive, Ajax can save money by using the excavated soil to build the terraces.

PROPOSAL B: TERRACES AND RIPRAPPED WATERWAY

Proposal B includes the same terraces as in proposal A, but the terraces flow into a riprapped channel going through the site and leading water beyond the boundaries of the property. A filter material must underlay the entire area that the riprap will cover (Minnesota Department of Transportation, 2005). Geotextile is the best material for this purpose. On top of this will be a 6-inch layer of granular filter material of uniform thickness over the prepared foundation. With geotextile, the foundation surface must be smooth and free of stones or other debris, and the fabric must not be torn during application. The riprap rocks should be placed from the bottom of the waterway to the top to achieve a uniform size distribution, with the smallest percent of void space possible. When completed, the riprap should not be less than 95% of the specified thickness.

PROPOSAL C: BURIED PIPELINE

A buried pipeline is the least optimal choice for the site. Methods

O'Bryan provides an analysis of three proposals, giving an overview of how each proposal would be implemented and recommending one.

First- and second-level headings are centered in all capital letters.

O'Bryan uses USGS style for citing sources in the text.

O'Bryan 5

of erosion control that are constructed aboveground are preferred because it is much easier to perform maintenance on them. There is no room for error in the design and construction of a buried pipeline. Also, in the site area, clay makes up a large percentage of the soil; the shrink-swell potential of the soil could later damage the pipes. Pipelines are also just as expensive as riprap. For this method, a retaining wall would be constructed of gabion baskets, which are more flexible than concrete and allow for the possibility of establishing vegetation in the spaces. As with the riprap plan, an erosion control blanket is required under the gabion to prevent scouring. There are several drawbacks to the use of gabions. As Lynn Merill (2004) writes, quoting engineer Mark North, "'Gabions may not be appropriate for use in high-traffic areas' where people coming in contact with them run the risk of 'snagging their clothes on the wire.'" In addition, gabions can be very expensive.

GUIDELINES FOR CONSTRUCTION[1]

Geotextile material.—Geotextile material should be "woven, nonwoven, or knit fabric of polymeric filaments or yarns such as polypropylene, polyethylene, polyester, or polyamide formed into a stable network such that the filaments/yarns retain their relative position to each other" (Minnesota Department of Transportation, 2005, p. 907). If the geotextile is being used as an earth reinforcement or under riprap, all sewn seams on the fabric must meet strength requirements.

Erosion control blankets.—Erosion control blankets are designed to be used until vegetation can be established. There are nine different categories of blankets based on use longevity and flow velocity; use longevity ranges from 6-8 weeks through permanent. The category chosen should be specific to the method of construction and to the site. For example, if gabions are built and the flow velocity is calculated to be less than 6.5 ft/s, a category 6 erosion control blanket should be used. The blanket should be laid out parallel to the direction of flow, and adjacent blanket edges should overlap by at least 4 inches and should be stapled.

---

[1]All guidelines are based on Minnesota Department of Transportation, 2005, and Beasley and others, 1984, unless stated otherwise.

O'Bryan provides guidelines that should be followed for any of the three proposals. She uses a footnote to give the sources of her guidelines.

In USGS style, minor subheadings are indented and italicized, followed by a period and a dash.

O'Bryan uses a footnote for a general point related to the entire section.

O'Bryan 6

At the top of the slope, the blanket should be buried in a check slot, which should be backfilled and compacted. Within the channel, the blanket should be stapled every foot.

Silt fences.—No silt should be washed off-site, and the soil must be seeded if it is to be bare for more than 45 days. It is expected that silt fences will be required at some point during construction of any of the proposed plans. It is acceptable to use the standard machine-sliced silt fencing during site grading to keep sediment from moving. Each post of the silt fence should be secured by a minimum of five gun staples 1 inch long.

Excavation.—During excavation, a well-drained condition must be maintained through planned drainage facilities. Topsoil should be stockpiled and covered. If blasting is required, it must be conducted so that materials will not be thrown out of the area and will be easily recoverable. Excavations must have a secure uniformity in grade; if excavations fall below final grade, they must be done with the provision that they are subject to change.

Pipe installation.—Pipes should be installed to collect and discharge water infiltrating into the soil or accumulated in a subcut or to cut off or intercept groundwater flow. The pipes should be constructed of nonperforated threadless copper (TP) pipe. Minimum trench width should be the diameter of the pipe plus two times the diameter. All rocks within the trench should be removed. A fine filter aggregate layer of one pipe diameter should be laid in the bottom of the trench. If perforated pipe is used, it must be wrapped in geotextile. Pipes that will discharge at a constructed gabion wall should be installed so that small movements in the wall will not cause the pipes to separate.

Reseeding.—The purpose of reseeding the area is not just to beautify the landscape. Reseeding is also an effective erosion control method. The application of seed must be conducted with as much rigor and attention to detail as any construction project on the site will be carried out. The establishment of permanent vegetation requires soil tilling, liming, fertilizing, seeding, sodding, mulching, and any other work required to ensure that the plants survive to maturity. Proper planting times must be observed; until the time for seeding has arrived, previously

O'Bryan 7

mentioned methods of erosion control must be used. The recommended
temporary seeding mixture is mixture number 130; its seeding date varies
because this seed has 40% of both winter wheat and oats. The optimal
time for planting winter wheat is Aug. 1-Oct. 1, and for oats it is May 1-
Aug. 1. Other seed mixture numbers have different planting seasons, as

Tables are referred to in the text and are placed as close as possible to their text reference.

shown in table 1.

If rills or gullies have formed anywhere on the site, they should
be filled in prior to seeding and compacted so that they are approximately
the same density as the surrounding soil. The seed should be applied
according to the seed application rate for its mixture number (see
table 2). Hydroseeding is prohibited when wind speeds exceed 15 mph.
The traditional seed mixes (numbers 100-280) should be applied through
hydroseeding; native mixes, because of the shape of the seed, require a
native seed drill. In hydroseeding, seed must be uniformly distributed;
otherwise the area must be reseeded. The permanent seed mixture can be
applied to an area that is covered with a temporary seed mixture without
additional tillage or site preparation. The water-to-straw-bale ratio with
tackifier for mulch is 100 gallons to every 50-pound bale.

PROPOSAL A: DETAILS AND GENERAL SPECIFICATIONS

O'Bryan gives specific details about her recommended proposal.

Seeded terraces and waterway.—On this site, there will be 7 sets of
terraces 120 feet apart in the clayey silt soil and 6 sets of terraces 150 feet
apart in the silty clay soil. The terraces will have a 0.60% gradient. They
will begin at elevation 560 feet and will be 600 feet long, increasing by

Table number and title appear above the table. A headnote, in brackets, gives source information; it also can explain abbreviations or symbols.

Table 1. Planting seasons for seed

[From Minnesota Department of Transportation, 2005, table 2575-1, p. 712]

Seed mixture number	Spring	Fall
100	—	Aug. 1-Oct. 1
110	May 1-Aug. 1	—
150, 190	Apr. 1-July 20	July 20-Oct. 20
240, 250, 260, 270	Apr. 1-June 1	July 20-Sept. 20
280	Apr. 1-Sept. 1	—
310, 325, 328, 330, 340, 350	Apr. 15-July 20	Sept. 20-Oct. 20

O'Bryan 8

Table 2. Seed application rates
[From Minnesota Department of Transportation, 2005, table 2575-2, p. 716]

Seed mixture number	Application rate (lb/acre)
100, 110	100
159	40
190	60
240	75
250	70
260	100
270	120
280	50
310	82
325	84
328	88
330, 340, 350	84.5

28.5 feet at each terrace until they reach 1,000 feet in length at elevation 480 feet. Work should start at the base of the area and proceed upward. The terraces will flow into a larger grassed waterway approximately 1,200 feet long that intersects the site.

 The terraces will be grassed with a native harvest. The waterway will be lined with something comparable to C350 riprap replacement and will also be seeded with a native harvest. The native harvest should consist of seed harvests from stands within 25 miles of the area. Approximately 70% of the mixture should consist of big bluestem and/or Indian grass, though 50% would be acceptable. There should be at least five species of native grasses and 3% (by mass) of native forbs. Since this is to be a recreational area, it will be best not to use a variety of grass that needs seasonal burning unless the park can be closed without financial repercussions and without the fire damaging any infrastructure erected at a later time. The application of herbicides seasonally (spring or summer) is acceptable though not encouraged, as runoff could harm fish and wildlife.

In USGS style, most numbers are expressed as numerals.

Erosion barrier.—The developer may not disturb more than 14,400 ft^2 at a time in the clayey silt soil or more than 22,500 ft^2 at a time in the silty clay soil without erecting an erosion barrier such as a silt fence on the downslope side. The bare soil above the work area should be stabilized by rocks and mulch at the end of each workday. The developer should create and maintain a covered stockpile of topsoil. If soil is going to be left bare for more than 45 days, it must be seeded. Idle areas should be seeded as soon as possible after grading or within 7 days. The seed should be mixture number 130, consisting of 40% oats, 40% winter wheat, 10% rye grass, and 10% alfalfa, annual. Compacted soils in the area should be deep-tilled to a depth of 18-24 inches to allow for deep root penetration. Six or more inches of organic compost should be laid on top of this and tilled into the top 10 inches of soil.

Lake.—Although a collection system for the runoff water was not a requirement for this proposal, a lake has several advantages and is not prohibitively expensive. It will collect drainage from the constructed waterway, it will attract wildlife to the area and enhance the appeal to visitors, and it can serve as a recreational fishing hole.

Other vegetation.—Revegetation should occur at the end of the major construction phase and should focus not only on establishing grasses in the area but also on planting other forms of vegetation. Some of the options for native plants that are readily available from nurseries are outlined in the "Shoreline Stabilization Handbook" (Northwest Regional Planning Commission, 2004). They include trees, shrubs, herbaceous plants, ferns, and vines. It is preferred that these be native to the area, such as Kentucky bluegrass, and not European or Asian in origin. While the European and Asian grasses have traditionally been used in American landscaping, they tend to have much smaller rooting zones and are not suitable for effective erosion control; they also require more effort to grow in this site soil. Native grasses would not have these problems and would be less expensive to maintain. Shrubs such as sumac, gray dogwood, wild rose, fragrant sumac, and hazelnut are also preferable because they have a dense, low-spreading growth pattern and are attractive.

Proposals usually provide itemized costs for the client.

Cost estimates.—The basic construction of Proposal A will cost Ajax $37,034-79,034. Additional costs of approximately $608,000 would provide

O'Bryan 10

for recovery of the runoff water and enhance the overall appearance and
appeal of the area.

DIMENSIONS

Disturbed area	216,283.5 yd^2
Total area	333,330 yd^2
Undisturbed area	117,046.5 yd^2

BASIC COSTS

Terraces	$	15,034.00
Grassed waterway		4,000.00
1-acre lake		18,000.00-60,000.00
TOTAL BASIC COSTS............................		$37,034.00-79,034.00

ADDITIONAL COSTS (OPTIONAL)

Hydroseeding, tackifier not required	$175,570.00
Hydroseeding, tackifier required	432,567.00
TOTAL ADDITIONAL COSTS................................	$608,137.00

CONCLUSION

While not the lowest-cost method of erosion control, proposal A
meets all the goals of the project and creates an aesthetically pleasing
and natural park atmosphere. The constructed appearance of the heavier
erosion control options such as riprap and gabions would not mesh well
with natural foliage. Such constructions also would not allow for aquatic
life, one of the stated goals of the project. Heavy vegetation with the more
aesthetic option of terraces is the correct choice in this situation. Native
grasses not only will facilitate slope stabilization because of their deep
rooting zones but also will attract birds and other wildlife, which would in
turn draw wildlife enthusiasts into the park.

A good model for the proposed park is the Rachel Carson National
Wildlife Refuge in Maine. While the type of land that is being protected
in Maine is different from the land found on the Kentucky site, the Maine
park combines the elements Ajax is seeking in its new park: a wildlife
refuge, full of native plants, and a recreational area. The Maine park has
trails throughout so that visitors have many different views of the beauty
of the site. It also offers fishing and hunting and appeals to many different
demographics. Ajax should consider this park as an ideal model.

In her conclusion,
O'Bryan states
again why she
recommends
proposal A. She
ends with a
paragraph that
speaks plainly to
connect with her
readers.

O'Bryan 11

REFERENCES

Beasley, R.P., Gregory, J.M., and McCarty, T.R., 1984, Erosion and sediment
pollution control (2d ed.): Ames, Iowa, Iowa State University Press,
354 p.

Merill, L., 2004, Multitalented and versatile—gabions in stormwater
management and erosion control: Erosion Control, v. 11, no. 3,
http://www.erosioncontrol.com/may-june-2004/gabions-cages
-erosion.aspx.

Metropolitan Council, July 2001, Soil erosion control—vegetative
methods, *in* Minnesota urban small sites BMP manual: St. Paul,
Minn., Metropolitan Council Environmental Services, http://www
.metrocouncil.org/environment/Watershed/BMP/CH3_RPPSoilVeget
.pdf.

Minnesota Department of Transportation, 2005, Standard specifications for
construction: St. Paul, Minn., Minnesota Department of
Transportation, http://www.dot.state.mn.us/pre-letting/spec/2005
/2557-2582.pdf.

Northwest Regional Planning Commission, 2004, The shoreline stabilization
handbook for Lake Champlain and other inland lakes: St. Albans, Vt.,
Northwest Regional Planning Commission, http://nsgd.gso.uri.edu
/lcsg/lcsgh04001.pdf.

U.S. Fish and Wildlife Service, 2008, Rachel Carson National Wildlife
Refuge: Wells, Maine, U.S. Fish and Wildlife Service, http://www.fws
.gov/northeast/rachelcarson.

D7 Writing in history

Historians analyze the information available to them to develop theories about past events, experiences, ideas, and movements. Depending on their interests, historians may consider a variety of issues and sources related to economics, politics, social issues, science, the military, gender, the family, or popular culture.

Historians do not simply record what happened at a particular time; rather, they attempt to explain *why* or *how* events occurred and to place those events in a larger context. For example, a historian writing about women in the British military during World War II would not simply describe the positions women held in the armed forces; through an analysis of the available information, the historian might develop a theory about why women were authorized to hold certain jobs and not others and how changes to women's roles affected the evolution of the women's rights movement in the decades that followed.

D7-a Determine your audience and their needs in history.

Historians write for diverse audiences. History scholars research and write books, articles, textbooks, Web sites, and film scripts for peers, teachers, and students. They also write for the general public, nonspecialists who are interested in history and may subscribe to history magazines or make frequent trips to museums. Amateur historians, often called "local historians," do genealogical or community research for a specific audience.

When you write in history, keep in mind that your audience appreciates an author who is knowledgeable and has done thorough research. Use multiple sources and cite your sources fully to assure your readers that your sources are credible. Because primary sources offer important evidence, include photos, maps, letters, or facsimiles. For example, if you are writing a newsletter article about a slave auction that occurred during the 1850s, you might add a picture of the poster that was used to advertise that auction.

D7-b Recognize the forms of writing in history.

Writing in history combines narrative (a description of what happened) and interpretation (an analysis of why events occurred). Historians ask questions that do not have obvious answers and analyze a variety of sources to draw conclusions.

When you take courses in history, you may be asked to write any of the following kinds of documents:

- critical essays
- book reviews
- research papers
- historiographic essays

Critical essays

For some assignments, you will be asked to write a short, critical essay in which you look at a document or group of documents—or perhaps a historical argument written by a scholar. For example, if you were studying the US decision to send troops to Vietnam, you might be asked to analyze one or more of John F. Kennedy's speeches and put forth a theory about why Kennedy chose to authorize the initial troop deployments. In the same course, you might be asked to read a journal article by a scholar analyzing Kennedy's decision and assess the way that scholar uses evidence to support his or her conclusion.

Book reviews

Because historians view their own work as part of an ongoing scholarly conversation, they value the serious discussion of the work of other scholars in the field. In some courses, you may be asked to write a book review analyzing the logic and accuracy of a scholarly work or of several works on the same topic. When you write a book review, you will have to make judgments about how much background information to provide about the book so that your readers will be able to understand and appreciate your critique.

Research papers

When you write a research paper in any course, you are expected to pose a question and examine the available evidence to find an answer to that question. In history courses, a research paper will generally focus on *why* and *how* questions that can be answered using a combination of sources. If you were studying the Vietnam War, you might ask how the rhetoric of the Cold War shaped John F. Kennedy's early Vietnam policy. To answer this question, you might look at government documents from the Kennedy administration, press coverage of Kennedy's foreign policy, Kennedy's own writings, and interviews with those who were involved in policymaking. If you were interested in the role of women in the military during World War II, you might ask why the British government supported the expansion of women's roles in ways that the US government did not.

Historiographic essays

Historiography is the study by historians of how history is written. When you write a historiographic essay, you think about the methods by which other historians have drawn their conclusions. If you were writing a historiographic essay about how the Cold War affected John F. Kennedy's policies, you would analyze how other historians have answered this question. What assumptions or biases influenced their choice and interpretation of sources? What methods shaped their work?

D7-C Know the questions historians ask.

Historians generally ask *how* and *why* questions. Other, more basic questions such as *What happened?* and *Who was involved?* will contribute answers to inform the broader, more controversial questions. Historians choose their questions by considering their own interests, the relevance to the ongoing discussions among scholars, and the availability of sources on the topic. The answer to any one of the following questions could form the basis of a thesis for a history paper.

- What role did nationalism play in the breakup of Yugoslavia in the early 1990s?
- Why did the US Congress decide to grant women the vote?
- How did the Salem witch trials (1692–93) differ from the Salzburg witch trials (1675–90)?
- Why did the Roman Empire collapse?

D7-d Understand the kinds of evidence historians use.

As investigators of the past, historians rely on both primary sources and secondary sources. Primary sources are materials from the historical period being studied—government documents, numerical data, speeches, diaries, letters, and maps. Secondary sources are materials produced after the historical period that interpret or synthesize historical events. The same source can function as either a primary or a secondary source depending on what you are writing about. For example, a newspaper article about Slobodan Milosevic's decision to defend himself during his war crimes trial would be a secondary source in an essay about why Milosevic made this decision. The same article, however, would be a primary source in an essay about newspaper coverage of Milosevic's war crimes trial.

Following are some of the ways historians use evidence.

- For a research paper about the role of women in the British military during World War II, you might find evidence in women's diaries and letters. If you were interested in how the government decided to create women's military services, you could consult records of parliamentary debates or correspondence between military and government leaders. You could also find numerous books by other scholars with information on the topic.

- For a research paper about attitudes toward Prohibition in different parts of the United States, you might consult regional newspapers or correspondence between politicians and their constituents. You might also find numerical data on liquor sales and Prohibition violations to support a hypothesis about regional attitudes.

- For a review of several books about the causes of the Tiananmen Square massacre, your evidence would come from the books themselves as well as other respected sources on the topic.

D7-e   Become familiar with writing conventions in history.

No matter what topic they are writing about, historians agree on some general conventions.

- Historians value counterargument. To draw a conclusion about why or how something happened, historians must weigh conflicting theories and interpretations carefully and judiciously. In an essay answering the question of why the US Congress passed the Nineteenth Amendment, you might conclude that politicians truly believed that women should have the right to vote. But you would also need to account for the failure of the same legislation several years earlier. Did politicians change their minds? Or were other factors at work?

- Historians conduct research. Historians, like detectives or forensic specialists, look for explanations by assessing the available evidence rather than relying on assumptions or personal opinions. They look for multiple sources of evidence to confirm their theories, and they avoid value judgments.

- Historians write in the past tense when they are focusing on past events, ideas, and movements. They use the present tense (*Goodman's book reveals new evidence*) or present perfect tense (*Olson has vividly depicted the political scene*) when talking about the contents of another writer's work.

- Historians credit the scholarship of others. Historians are aware that they are joining an existing scholarly conversation, and they place great importance on citing the ideas of other scholars.

D7-f Use the CMS (*Chicago*) system in writing in history.

Writers in history typically use the style guidelines of *The Chicago Manual of Style* (CMS) for formatting their papers, for citing sources in the text of their paper and in endnotes, and for listing sources in a bibliography at the end. CMS style is set forth in *The Chicago Manual of Style*, 16th ed. (Chicago: University of Chicago Press, 2010). (For more details, see the CMS documentation sections in your handbook.)

D7-g Sample student paper: Research essay

A history research paper generally focuses on a *how* or a *why* question, and it answers this question with an analysis of available sources. The student paper beginning on the next page was written for a course on the history of the industrial revolution in the United States. The student, Jenna Benjamin, used the style guidelines of *The Chicago Manual of Style* (CMS) to format her paper and to cite and list her sources.

Title page consists of a descriptive title and the writer's name in the center of the page and the course number, instructor, and date at the bottom of the page.

Wage Slavery or True Independence?
Women Workers in the Lowell, Massachusetts,
Textile Mills, 1820-1850

Jenna Benjamin

American History 200, Section 4
Professor Jones
May 22, XXXX

Marginal annotations indicate CMS-style formatting and effective writing.

In 1813, New England merchant Francis Lowell introduced a new type of textile mill to Massachusetts that would have a permanent impact on family and village life. Over the next three decades, the transformation of home production to factory production of textiles would require a substantial labor force and would lead to the unprecedented hiring of thousands of women. The entrance of young women into the workforce sparked a passionate debate about whether factory work exploited young women and adversely affected society. The young women who worked in the mills received low pay for hard work and had little free time.[1] Were these women victims of the factory system? What was the long-term impact of their experiences? An analysis of the evidence reveals that rather than being exploited, these women workers shaped their experience for their own purposes and actively expanded the opportunities for women.

In the late eighteenth century, great changes in the production of textiles were taking place in England, with a transition from home production to factories using machines and employing children to do most of the work. Conditions in the factories were very bad, and stories of dark and dangerous mills reinforced Americans' prejudices against industrialization.[2] Meanwhile, New Englanders still spun yarn at home and some also wove their own cloth, mostly for their own families. Much of this work was done by women. A spinning wheel was a possession of almost every household.[3] But in the first two decades of the nineteenth century, a slow shift took place in New England from home to factory production.

Some American merchants, like Samuel Slater and Francis Cabot Lowell, began to envision an American textile industry. The first mills they built in the United States were in rural villages and employed whole families, not just children. Since the textile mills hired whole families who already lived in the villages, family and village life was not greatly altered.[4]

A dramatic change in textile production, however, came from a new machine, the power loom, and a new mechanized mill, built first in Waltham, Massachusetts, in 1813 by Francis Lowell and a small group of wealthy Boston merchants.[5] Waltham was not a village with a textile mill in it; it became a "mill town" in which the factory dominated the economic

Page header contains the writer's name followed by the page number. Since the title page is counted in the numbering, the first text page is numbered 2.

Introduction frames a debatable issue.

Research questions focus the essay.

Statement of thesis.

Section provides background about the historical period.

Historians write in the past tense when describing past events.

Benjamin 3

life of a rapidly growing city. Most significantly, the workers in Lowell's mill were not local families but individuals who came from great distances to live and work in the new mill town. When Lowell died in 1817, his business partners spread the new factory system to other places, notably a town on the Merrimack and Concord Rivers twenty-seven miles from Boston; in honor of their friend, they named the town Lowell. It soon became the biggest mill town in the nation, with more than a dozen large integrated mills using mechanical looms.[6]

Note numbers in text refer to endnotes at the end of the paper.

The growth of Lowell between 1821 and 1840 was unprecedented.[7] A rapidly developing textile industry like the one at Lowell needed more and more people to work the machines in the factories. The mill owners, aware of the negative view of English mill towns, decided to create a community where workers would live in solid, clean housing rather than slums. For their workers, they looked to a large group of people whose labor was not absolutely necessary to the New England farm economy— hundreds (later thousands) of young women who lived on the farms but who could be persuaded to come to Lowell and work in the mills.[8]

Topic sentence signals a transition to a specific discussion of the women workers.

Several factors in the social and economic history of New England made this group of workers available. Population growth and scarcity of land to pass down to younger generations of sons caused many New England farmers to send their sons to work on neighboring farms or as apprentices to craftsmen in towns or villages.[9] In addition, the position of women (wives and, especially, daughters) in the family was an inferior one. Adult, property-holding males were citizens with full civil rights, but the same was not true for women *of any age*. Wives had no legal rights, and daughters had no independence. Daughters were bound by social conventions to obey their fathers and rarely were able to earn money of their own. Even travel away from home was unusual. Although the family could not have functioned without the labor of wives and daughters at field work, food preparation, cleaning, washing, and so on, women gained no independent income or freedom as a result. For some young women, their subordinate position in family and society gave them an incentive to embrace the opportunities offered by mill work. Unlike the limited occupation of teaching, which was poorly paid and lasted for only a few months a year, the new mill work was steady, and it paid well.[10]

Benjamin 4

Hiring young women, of course, met strong resistance from fathers
who saw their role as protecting their daughters and preparing them
for marriage.[11] To confront this resistance, the mill owners created
boardinghouses around the mills where groups of girls—ranging in age
from fifteen to mid-twenties—lived and took their meals under the care
of a housekeeper, usually an older woman. Strict boardinghouse rules
were laid down by each company (see fig. 1). Moreover, the girls would

> ### REGULATIONS
> FOR THE
> ### BOARDING HOUSES
> OF THE
> # MIDDLESEX COMPANY.
>
> THE tenants of the Boarding Houses are not to board, or permit
> any part of their houses to be occupied by any person except those in
> the employ of the Company.
>
> They will be considered answerable for any improper conduct in
> their houses, and are not to permit their boarders to have company at
> unseasonable hours.
>
> The doors must be closed at ten o'clock in the evening, and no
> one admitted after that time without some reasonable excuse.
>
> The keepers of the Boarding Houses must give an account of the
> number, names, and employment of their boarders, when required;
> and report the names of such as are guilty of any improper conduct, or
> are not in the regular habit of attending public worship.
>
> The buildings and yards about them must be kept clean and in
> good order, and if they are injured otherwise than from ordinary use,
> all necessary repairs will be made, and charged to the occupant.
>
> It is indispensable that all persons in the employ of the Middlesex
> Company should be vaccinated who have not been, as also the families
> with whom they board; which will be done at the expense of the
> Company.
>
> **SAMUEL LAWRENCE, Agent.**
>
> JOEL TAYLOR, PRINTER, Daily Courier Office.

Fig. 1. Each mill company established strict rules for the boardinghouses
where its women workers lived. (American Textile History Museum, Lowell,
Massachusetts.)

A primary source
(a document)
provides concrete
evidence and adds
historical interest.

A caption below
the writer's visual
evidence gives the
figure number, a
brief description,
and information
about the source.

(*Source:* Reprinted by permission of the American Textile History Museum,
Lowell, Massachusetts.)

never grow into a permanent working class, as it was expected that they
would return to their homes for visits and after a year or two would go
back to their villages permanently.[12] The mill owners did not advertise
for help. They sent recruiters into the countryside to assure parents that
their daughters would live under strict supervision in the boardinghouses
and at work and that their behavior would be monitored. The owners'
efforts were successful: over the years, thousands of young women took the
long trip by stagecoach or wagon from their rural homes to mill towns like
Lowell.[13]

Benjamin introduces evidence that appears to contradict her thesis (counterargument).

Besides having to adjust to living in a city in a strange house with
a dozen or more other girls, the young women had to get used to the
rigorous rules and long hours at the mills.[14] Mill work was an opportunity,
but it also was hard work. The girls worked an average of twelve hours a
day. The mills operated six days a week, so the only day off was Sunday,
part of which was usually spent at church. Thus free time was confined to
two or three hours in the evening and to Sunday afternoon.[15] For many,
however, this was still more leisure (and more freedom) than they would
have had at home.

Despite a workday that took up fourteen hours, including time spent
traveling to and from their houses for meals, most of the young women
did not find the work very strenuous or particularly dangerous. As the mill
owners had promised, Lowell did not resemble the grimy, packed mill towns
of England.[16] Still, the work was tedious and confining, with the girls
doing the same operation over and over again under the watchful eye of
the overseer.[17]

Benjamin develops a response to the counterargument, with strong evidence for her thesis.

The young women earned an average of three to four dollars a week,
from which their board of $1.25 a week was deducted. At that time, no
other jobs open to women paid as well.[18] Three or four dollars a week
was enough to pay board, send badly needed money home, and still have
enough left over for new clothes once in a while. Many women mill workers
even established savings accounts, and some eventually left Lowell with
several hundred dollars, something they never could have done at home.[19]

Details about the beneficial effects on the young mill workers come from primary and secondary sources.

Even though their free time was very limited, the young women
engaged in a variety of activities. In the evenings, they wrote letters
home, entertained visitors (though there was little privacy), repaired their

Benjamin 6

clothing, and talked about friends and relatives and also about conditions
in the mills. They could go out to the shops, especially clothing shops.
The mill girls at Lowell prided themselves on a wardrobe that, at least on
Sunday, was not inferior to that of the wives of prosperous citizens.[20] In
addition, they attended evening courses that enabled them to extend their
education beyond their few years of schooling. They also attended lectures
and read novels and essays. So strong was the girls' interest in reading that
many mills put up signs warning "No reading in the mills."[21] Some young
women even began writing. Determined to challenge the idea that mill girls
were mindless drones of the factory and lacked the refinement to ultimately
be good wives, about seventy-five mill girls and women contributed in
the 1840s to publications featuring stories and essays by the workers
themselves.[22]

Benjamin
paraphrases
information from a
secondary source,
a late-nineteenth-
century book.

The best known of these publications was the *Lowell Offering*. The
Offering avoided sensitive issues about working conditions, but the women
controlled the content of the publication and wrote on subjects (family,
courtship, fashion, morality, nature) that interested them.[23] A few of the
Offering writers even went on to literary careers, not the kind of future
that most people expected of factory workers. Charles Dickens toured the
mills in 1842 and later said of the girls' writing: "Of the merits of the
Lowell Offering, as a literary production, I will only observe . . . that it will
compare advantageously with a great many English annuals."[24]

Direct quotation
provides evidence
from the period.

Though the *Offering* was a sign that something unusual was
happening in this factory town, the women still worked in an industry that
caused them hardship. By the 1830s, tensions in the mills had begun to
rise as the companies became more interested in profits and less concerned
about their role as protectors of their young workers. Factory owners,
observing a decline in the price of their cloth and an increase in unsold
inventories, decided to lower their workers' wages.[25] When the reduction was
announced in February 1834, the women workers circulated petitions among
themselves pledging to stop work (or "turn out") if wages were lowered.[26]
When the leader of the petition drive at one mill was fired, many of the
women left work and marched to the other mills to call out their workers.
It is estimated that one-sixth of all women mill workers walked out as a
result. The strikers wrote another petition stating that "we will not go back

into the mills to work until our wages are continued . . . as they have been."[27]

Although the "turn out" was brief and did not achieve its purpose, it demonstrated that the women workers did not accept the owners' view that they were minors under the owners' benevolent care. The sense of independence gained by factory work and cash wages led them to reject the idea that they were mere factory hands. Petitions referred to their "unquestionable rights" and to "the spirit of our patriotic ancestors, who preferred privation to bondage." One petition ended, "We are free, we would remain in possession of what kind providence has bestowed upon us, and remain *daughters of free men still.*"[28] This language indicates that the women did not think of themselves as laborers complaining about low wages. They were free citizens of a republic and deserved respect as such. Many young women left the mills and went home when mill work came to seem more like "slavery" than independence (a comparison that appeared in the petitions). In 1836, another effort to lower wages led to an even larger "turn out."[29] The willingness of these young women to challenge the authority of the mill owners is a sign that their new lives had given them a feeling of personal strength and solidarity with one another.[30]

Economic recession in the late 1830s and early 1840s led to the layoff of hundreds more women workers. In the 1840s and 1850s, the mill owners tried to maintain profits by increasing the workload and abandoning paternalism toward their workers. To save money, the companies stopped building boardinghouses.[31] The look of Lowell changed as well. Mill buildings took up more of the green space that had been part of the original town plan. By 1850, Lowell did indeed look something like an English mill town.

As conditions in the mills and in the city declined, young New England women were replaced by young Irish immigrants escaping the famine and the poor living conditions in Ireland. Slowly, Lowell became just another industrial city. It was dirty and overcrowded, and its mills were beginning to look run-down.[32]

By 1850, an era had passed. But from the 1820s to the 1840s, the majority of the textile workers were young women who helped make possible the industrialization of New England at the same time as they expanded

Benjamin analyzes the quotation to show how it supports the paragraph's main point.

Strong evidence supports the paper's thesis.

Concluding paragraph opens with a brief restatement of part of the thesis.

Benjamin 8

their own opportunities. These early mill workers became models for later women reformers and radicals who raised the banner for equal rights for women in more and more areas of life. The independent mill girls of the 1830s and 1840s resisted pressures from their employers, gained both freedom and maturity by living and working on their own, and showed an intense desire for independence and learning.[33] Great fortunes were made from the textile mills of that era, but within those mills a generation of young women gained something even more precious: a sense of self-respect.

Conclusion considers the broader implications of the thesis.

Notes

Endnotes begin on
a new page. Sources
are cited in CMS
(*Chicago*) style.
Complete source
information is also
listed in the
bibliography.

1. Caroline F. Ware, *The Early New England Cotton Manufacture* (Boston: Houghton Mifflin, 1931), 4-8; Barbara M. Tucker, *Samuel Slater and the Origins of the American Textile Industry, 1790-1860* (Ithaca, NY: Cornell University Press, 1984), 38-41.

2. Tucker, *Samuel Slater*, 33-40.

Citation of a journal
article from a
database. Section
locator is used
for unpaginated
source.

3. Thomas Dublin, *Women at Work: The Transformation of Work and Community in Lowell, Massachusetts, 1826-1860* (New York: Columbia University Press, 1979), 14; Adrienne D. Hood, "The Gender Division of Labor in the Production of Textiles in Eighteenth-Century Rural Pennsylvania," *Journal of Social History* 27, no. 3 (1994), "Spinning as Women's Work" section, Academic OneFile (A15324645).

4. Tucker, *Samuel Slater*, 79, 85, 99-100, 111; Barbara M. Tucker, "The Family and Industrial Discipline in Ante-Bellum New England," *Labor History* 21, no. 1 (1979): 56-60.

5. Robert F. Dalzell, *Enterprising Elite: The Boston Associates and the World They Made* (Cambridge, MA: Harvard University Press, 1987), 26-30; Tucker, *Samuel Slater*, 111-16.

Second reference to
a source includes the
author's name, a
shortened title, and
the page numbers.

6. Tucker, *Samuel Slater*, 116-17.

7. Dublin, *Women at Work*, 19-21, 133-35.

8. Ibid., 26, 76; Benita Eisler, ed., *The "Lowell Offering": Writings by New England Mill Women, 1840-1845* (Philadelphia: Lippincott, 1977), 15-16.

First line of each
note is indented ½".
All notes are
single-spaced, with
double-spacing
between them.
(Some instructors
may prefer
double-spacing
throughout.)

9. Christopher Clark, "The Household Economy: Market Exchange and the Rise of Capitalism in the Connecticut Valley, 1800-1860," *Journal of Social History* 13, no. 2 (1979): 175-76, http://www.jstor.org/stable /3787339; Gail Fowler Mohanty, "Handloom Outwork and Outwork Weaving in Rural Rhode Island, 1810-1821," *American Studies* 30, no. 2 (1989): 42-43, 48-49.

10. Eisler, *"Lowell Offering,"* 16, 193; Clark, "Household Economy," 178-79; Dalzell, *Enterprising Elite*, 33.

Primary source
(Robinson)
reprinted in a
secondary source.

11. On the influence of patriarchy, see Tucker, *Samuel Slater*, 25-26; Harriet H. Robinson, *Loom and Spindle; Or, Life among the Early Mill Girls* (1898), reprinted in *Women of Lowell* (New York: Arno Press, 1974), 194; Barbara Welter, "The Cult of True Womanhood," *American Quarterly* 18, no. 2, pt. 1 (1966): 151, 170-71.

Benjamin 12

Bibliography

Bartlett, Elisha. *A Vindication of the Character and Condition of the Females Employed in the Lowell Mills.* 1841. Reprinted in *Women of Lowell.* New York: Arno Press, 1974.

A Citizen of Lowell. *Corporations and Operatives: Being an Exposition of the Condition [of] Factory Operatives and a Review of the "Vindication," by Elisha Bartlett, MD.* 1843. Reprinted in *Women of Lowell.* New York: Arno Press, 1974.

Clark, Christopher. "The Household Economy: Market Exchange and the Rise of Capitalism in the Connecticut Valley, 1800-1860." *Journal of Social History* 13, no. 2 (1979): 169-89. http://www.jstor.org/stable/3787339.

Dalzell, Robert F. *Enterprising Elite: The Boston Associates and the World They Made.* Cambridge, MA: Harvard University Press, 1987.

Dublin, Thomas. *Women at Work: The Transformation of Work and Community in Lowell, Massachusetts, 1826-1860.* New York: Columbia University Press, 1979.

Eisler, Benita, ed. *The "Lowell Offering": Writings by New England Mill Women, 1840-1845.* Philadelphia: Lippincott, 1977.

"Factory Rules from the Handbook to Lowell, 1848." Illinois Labor History Society. Center for Law and Computers, Chicago-Kent School of Law. Accessed May 12, 2006. http://www.kentlaw.edu/ilhs/lowell.html.

Hood, Adrienne D. "The Gender Division of Labor in the Production of Textiles in Eighteenth-Century Rural Pennsylvania." *Journal of Social History* 27, no. 3 (1994). Academic OneFile (A15324645).

Larcom, Lucy. "Among Lowell Mill-Girls: A Reminiscence." 1881. Reprinted in *Women of Lowell.* New York: Arno Press, 1974.

Mohanty, Gail Fowler. "Handloom Outwork and Outwork Weaving in Rural Rhode Island, 1810-1821." *American Studies* 30, no. 2 (1989): 41-68.

Robinson, Harriet H. *Loom and Spindle; Or, Life among the Early Mill Girls.* 1898. Reprinted in *Women of Lowell.* New York: Arno Press, 1974.

Sins of Our Mothers. Boston: PBS Video, 1988. Videocassette.

Stearns, Bertha Monica. "Early Factory Magazines in New England: The *Lowell Offering* and Its Contemporaries." *Journal of Economic and Business History* (1930): 685-705.

D8   Writing in music

Musicians and musicologists—those who study, analyze, and interpret music—write about music for themselves or for larger audiences. Your instructor might ask you to keep a journal to record your impressions and ideas about concerts you attend. If you are a music student, you might write personal reflections about works that you are preparing for performance. Other kinds of writing are intended to inform or educate general audiences. They include reviews of performances and press releases that are published in newspapers, blogs, or other publications. More specialized publications are scholarly journals and concert program notes.

If you are a student learning how to write about music, you will need to train yourself to listen actively rather than passively. Passive listening means just enjoying a performance or recording. This kind of listening is certainly a valid way to hear music, but to write about music you must become more aware of what you are hearing. You must intentionally listen for certain qualities in the music. Active listening also involves learning about the background of a composer or musician to deepen your understanding of the music. As an active listener, you can observe how the audience responds during a performance, and you can analyze and critique the performance as you listen. To help you become a more active listener, your instructor might take your class on field trips to concerts so you can experience a variety of performances. You might attend a classical symphony concert, a chamber music performance, a recital showcasing the talents of a single performer, or a concert by a rock band or a jazz ensemble.

D8-a   Determine your audience and their needs in music.

Audiences for music writers include professional musicians, music historians, and researchers, teachers, and students. They read scholarly or teaching journals to learn about new analyses or interpretations of musical compositions and about methods that other musicians, researchers, or teachers are using. Other audiences may include members of the general public, who read reviews of performances in newspapers or on Web sites to help them decide whether to attend concerts. Serious concertgoers read reviews after they attend a performance as a way of helping them think more about their experience at the concert. Audiences attending performances read the printed programs to learn about the biographies of composers and the histories of pieces they will hear. Some readers are in businesses, government agencies, or nonprofit organizations that fund musicians and arts groups. They read grant proposals written by researchers, musicians, teachers, and even students who are seeking funds to support their study or practice of music.

Readers in the field of music want to know the writer's opinion, but they expect the writing to contain more than just statements of personal taste. If the piece of writing is a music review, readers want the writer to evaluate the performance with specific details and examples to justify the writer's opinion. Because the discipline of music is a diverse field with a very long history, understanding one composer, work, or performer requires making connections to others in the field. All readers expect writers about music to make references to other composers, styles, or musicians.

D8-b Recognize the forms of writing in music.

When you take courses in music, you may be asked to write any of the following:

- response papers
- program notes
- press releases
- concert reviews
- journal articles
- grant proposals

Response papers

A response paper is your personal reflection on a piece of music, a composer, a performance, or your own progress as a musician. Your instructor may ask you to write the paper as a brief assignment or as part of a journal that you keep during the course. The purpose of personal response is to brainstorm some initial ideas or to reflect on a work you are studying or a concert you attended. These writing activities will help you generate topics for larger, more formal projects. To help you focus your attention on particular elements of a performance, your instructor may provide questions you can use in forming your response. Your instructor might assign a response paper after you attend a concert and then later require a concert review using your response paper as a starting point. Thus a response paper can help you move from your immediate reactions to a more objective piece of writing. To be sure that your responses are useful for later assignments, make them detailed and thorough. Avoid simply writing that you like or dislike a particular work or performer. Instead, provide details that illustrate exactly why you have that particular reaction.

Program notes

When people attend a formal concert or a recital, they are usually given a program that lists the pieces they will hear and describes those pieces so they can understand and appreciate the music they will hear. Those descriptions are called *program notes*. A program note usually includes a biographical profile of the composer, background information about the composer's historical period, some mention of the first performance of the piece with a list or survey of major performances, and a description of the piece. The description will guide audience members through the performance, describing what they can expect to hear in each section of the piece. One kind of program note is a profile of each performer, describing the performer's major accomplishments and listing schools attended and major past performances. It may also give a brief discography, a listing of recordings that the performer has made professionally. Writing program notes will require you to do some research so you can provide the information readers expect to enhance their enjoyment and understanding of the performance. Think of program notes as small research papers that teach your readers about the music they are going to listen to.

Press releases

A press release is a brief document of no more than 250 words announcing an upcoming musical event to the general public. It is written by the event's organizers and distributed locally for publication in newspapers, in magazines, and on Web sites and as announcements on radio and television. Begin a press release with a one- or two-sentence statement giving the most important information about the event: what it is, who the main performers will be, and the time, date, and location of the event. Your press release can continue with a description of the composers and performers who will be featured. The press release should conclude with any other relevant information such as cost, parking, and a Web site or phone number where readers can get more information.

Concert reviews

Concert reviews might be the most popular kind of writing about music. The reviewer attends a concert, listens actively and intently, and tells readers about the experience. When you write a concert review, begin by engaging your audience with one or more sentences that capture the quality and mood of the entire performance. Tell readers what composers and works were featured and who the performers were. Then write about each part of the concert. Briefly describe what was played and how it was played, stating your opinions about the music and the performers, with examples to illustrate your opinions. You might also integrate historical information about the composer, the piece of music, or the performers. Vivid words and active sentences will give readers a sense of how it felt to attend the performance.

Journal articles

Musicologists research and write about the history and literature of music, and they analyze works of music. They publish their interpretations in scholarly journals and present their work at professional conferences. You may be assigned a paper that involves research and musical analysis. A typical assignment might ask you to explain how a composition reflects its historical period or to trace trends in music in a time period or region. You might explore larger issues such as music in mass media or how technology has changed music. Your assignment might ask you to focus on a relatively unknown composer, performer, or work. If you are writing a journal article about the teaching of music, you might write a how-to paper that proposes an improved way to do something—how to rehearse a high school band more effectively, how to teach jazz improvisation, or how to start a school chamber music festival, for example. A paper of that type would involve reading articles, interviewing teachers and administrators, and using personal observations and experiences.

Grant proposals

Musicians and music teachers often apply for funding to support their projects. They might request money to purchase new equipment for their schools, to organize a summer workshop or camp, to travel to a library for research, or to attend a summer academy or workshop for intense study with well-known teachers. Whether you write a grant proposal on a form provided by the funding agency or draft your own, it typically includes several sections:

- an introduction that briefly describes the project and covers basic details about when, where, and how you expect the project to be achieved
- an outcomes section describing all the objectives you expect to attain with your project
- an itemized list of anticipated expenses

- a timeline section providing a schedule for completion, including deadlines for specific tasks
- a list of qualifications—the personal skills and experience that will enable you to complete the project
- a résumé

D8-c Know the questions musicians and musicologists ask.

Writers about music ask questions that guide them toward analysis and interpretation. The following are some questions that would lead to topics for research papers in music.

- In what ways do the symphonies of Brahms show the influence of earlier classical composers as well as the qualities of the Romantic period?
- How did rock and roll develop from earlier forms of music?
- How did changes in US society and mass media in the 1950s and 1960s influence the development of country music?
- What techniques of music composition and instrumentation has Beirut used to create his unique eastern European Gypsy–inspired brand of indie rock?
- What elements of electro-pop and folk does Ellie Goulding use most effectively in her hit single "Halcyon"?
- What challenges do symphony orchestras in the United States encounter, what are the causes of those challenges, and what are some effective strategies that cities have developed or could develop to build and sustain orchestras?

D8-d Understand the kinds of evidence musicians and musicologists use.

Musicians and musicologists use primary and secondary sources for evidence. A primary source is a music composition that the writer is analyzing or a concert or recording that the writer is reviewing. Secondary sources are books, articles, and Web sites about composers, musicians, or music.

The following are examples of the ways you might use evidence when you write about music.

- For program notes, you would use secondary sources for biographical material about the performer and historical information about the work of music to be performed. You might interview some of the performers (primary sources); for an original work, you might interview the composer, if possible.

- For a research paper tracing the development of Creole music in southern Louisiana, your primary sources could be songs representing different styles of Creole music and stages in the evolution of the music. Secondary sources would be books and other materials about the history of southern society and culture.

- For a review of a performance of Handel's *Messiah*, you would use specific moments from the concert itself as evidence to illustrate your opinions. You might mention how the conductor and the soloists interpreted particular parts of the piece and describe how sections of the orchestra and chorus performed. You might also note performers or moments from the performance that stood out because of their strengths or weaknesses.

D8-e Become familiar with writing conventions in music.

Musicians and musicologists agree on several conventions when they write.

- Musical compositions are known and categorized by detailed or specialized titles. For example, Beethoven's fifth symphony is Symphony no. 5 in C Minor, op. 67 (*op.* is the abbreviation for *opus*, or "work").

- Musicians and musicologists use a specialized vocabulary from music theory and history. Often that vocabulary includes words in Italian, German, or French. For example, movements of a symphony are known by their technical terms, such as the *adagio* section or the *allegro* movement.

- In reflective writing, the first-person pronoun *I* is acceptable. In a music review, it should be used sparingly so the review remains fair and analytical and does not seem to be merely a statement of personal taste. The first person can be used in grant proposals but not in press releases, program notes, or research papers in music.

- Writers use past tense to describe past events such as a composer's life or a performance. They use present tense when reviewing a recording or analyzing a work of music (for example, *In Nickel Creek's new song, the mandolin plays variations on an old folk tune*).

- Music writers use the active voice and active verbs to keep their writing lively and engaging.

D8-f Use the MLA system in writing in music.

Writers in music typically use the style guidelines of the Modern Language Association (MLA) to format a paper, to document sources within the paper, and to cite sources at the end of the paper. Those guidelines are set forth in the *MLA Handbook*, 8th edition (MLA, 2016). (For more details, see the MLA documentation sections in your handbook.)

In addition, specific information about writing in music can be found in D. Kern Holoman, *Writing about Music: A Style Sheet*, 2nd ed. (U of California P, 2008), and Jonathan Bellman, *A Short Guide to Writing about Music*, 2nd ed. (Longman, 2006).

D8-g Sample student paper: Concert review

A typical assignment in music courses is a review of a performance or a recording. Reviews appear in newspapers, in magazines, and on Web sites. The following student paper was written in a writing course for music majors and other students interested in music. The student, Tom Houston, attended a local concert for this assignment. He used the style guidelines in the *MLA Handbook* to format his paper and to cite and list his sources.

Tom Houston

Dr. Belland

MUS 291 W

27 February XXXX

Concert Review: Cincinnati Symphony Orchestra

The Cincinnati Symphony Orchestra performed a stunning concert Saturday evening, February 23, 2008. Those who came, filling Music Hall to almost two-thirds capacity, were immersed in what became a soul-searching musical experience provided by Maestro John Adams. The program selections and the exquisite performances offered the audience an opportunity to expand their appreciation for contemporary music.

Opening this energetic program was *Tod und Verklärung* ("Death and Transfiguration"), a tone poem by Richard Strauss. Following the Strauss, Adams led the orchestra in *On the Transmigration of Souls* and, after the intermission, *The Dharma at Big Sur*, both composed by Adams.

Strauss wrote *Tod und Verklärung*, a lively musical stampede, when he was just twenty-five years old. This seems to be a relatively young age to tackle such a profoundly heavy subject. In his preconcert talk, Adams observed that at the time Strauss was "a bit overwhelmed at his own orchestral virtuosity." Very effective in the introduction of this tone poem is the motif played by the timpani suggesting the faltering heartbeat of a dying elderly man. Then the music grows to a galloping romp—a very young Strauss's concept of the old man's entrance into Glory Land. At least this is the generally accepted interpretation. Listening carefully, one can hear partway through the Glory Land section the faltering heart still beating. Strauss might be giving us pre-death hallucinations followed by a slightly subdued entrance into heaven.

The orchestra under Adams gave an intense interpretation of this Strauss masterpiece. The gentle, soft voice usually brought to this orchestra by music director Paavo Järvi would have added a welcome intensified dramatic contrast to what was a rendition with merely adequate drama under Adams's baton.

It is strange to think of the Strauss piece as whimsical. It is a heavyweight probe into heavyweight matter. However, in his preconcert talk to the early concertgoers, Adams said that he added it to the program

---

Marginal annotations:

Writer's name and page number, flush right on every page.

Houston begins with the time and place of the concert and then gives his overall evaluation of the performance.

Houston provides context by listing the pieces on the program.

This section vividly describes the history and sound of the Strauss composition.

Houston evaluates how the orchestra performed the piece, giving supporting details from the performance.

Marginal annotations indicate MLA-style formatting and effective writing.

Houston 2

Transition contrasts
the first work
on the program
with the next work
to be discussed.

as "whimsy" but that it might not have been the most effective selection because it added more weight to an already heavy program. The truth of this comment became apparent during Adams's own *On the Transmigration of Souls*.

Houston provides
background,
description, and an
opinion about the
performance of the
second piece.

As the program notes by Richard E. Rodda indicate, *Transmigration* was originally written for and performed by the New York Philharmonic Orchestra in honor of the victims of the September 11, 2001, terrorist attacks. Adding to the orchestra the voices of the May Festival Chorus, the Cincinnati Children's Choir, and a prerecorded soundtrack, Adams transformed Music Hall into a cathedral. Adams's music avoids evoking the terrible scenes seen so many times, using as the text the simple, heartrending statements of both victims and their loved ones. Each poignant word was sung exquisitely, every phrase clearly understood through the appropriate musical dissonance of the orchestra.

Houston uses vivid
description to give
readers a sense of
what it was like to
attend the concert.

The depth of the significance of this work cannot be overstated. Adams captured this event not only through the souls of the victims but also through the souls of the surviving loved ones and the souls of all whose lives were forever changed that morning. The performance began with Adams standing motionless in a silent hall, and it ended with him standing motionless in a silent hall. It seemed almost a sacrilege to clap, but that is all an audience can do. It was like clapping after Communion. Soon Robert Porco, director of the May Festival Chorus, and Robyn Lana, director of the Cincinnati Children's Choir, appeared with Adams to accept a well-deserved tribute from the audience. This seemed to make the extended applause more appropriate and a welcome emotional release.

Houston provides
background about
an instrument and
music that might
be unfamiliar to
readers.

Following the intermission, violinist Leila Josefowicz appeared with the orchestra to perform Adams's *The Dharma at Big Sur*. This is quintessential Adams at his compositional best. The entire work sounds improvisational, especially the solo violin. The instrument, made especially for Josefowicz, is a six-string electric violin with a very wide range, so different from a traditional violin that the performer is required to learn new technique to play it. The music, moving beyond traditional Western tones, employs quarter, or in-between, tones, which slide up or down, giving a sound that is strange to Western, classically trained ears.

Houston 3

Josefowicz's enduring energy and technique, the controlled orchestral dissonance and extraordinarily equipped percussion section, and the leprechaunesque gyrations of Adams gave the audience an exciting listening and viewing experience.

Houston supports his opinion about the final piece with vivid details.

We Cincinnatians are traditionally a conservative people, preferring an orchestra to have a traditionally "full" or lush sound, but Adams composes on the leading crest of the wave of minimalism, a contemporary, spare sound that can make an audience uncomfortable. The concert Saturday night moved the Cincinnati audience a step or two forward.

The conclusion summarizes the general impact of the performance on the audience.

Houston 4

Works cited
list begins on a
new page and is
formatted in MLA
style.

Works Cited

Adams, John. Preconcert talk. Cincinnati Symphony Orchestra, Music Hall,
     Cincinnati, 23 Feb. 2008.

Cincinnati Symphony Orchestra. Conducted by John Adams, Music Hall,
     Cincinnati, 23 Feb. 2008. Performance.

Rodda, Richard E. "John Adams: *On the Transmigration of Souls*." Cincinnati
     Symphony Orchestra, 23 Feb. 2008. Program notes.

D9 Writing in nursing

Writing is an important tool in the education of nursing students as well as in the everyday workplaces of the profession. For students learning to become nurses, writing about specific nursing theories and practices, medical cases, and client experiences helps them better understand concepts and skills through research and analytical thinking.

For professional nurses, writing is a crucial means of communication with colleagues in the health care profession, communication that can improve the quality of care for patients, or *clients*, as they are increasingly called. Nurses write charts about their clients (a practice called *charting*), staff memos, patient education booklets, and policies for health care facilities. They may also contribute research articles to journals in the field or craft arguments to attempt to persuade decision makers to change or adopt a particular health care policy.

To write effectively in nursing, you need to support your claims with accurate client observations and current, researched evidence.

D9-a Determine your audience and their needs in nursing.

Nurses write for health care providers such as other nurses, patients or clients, and the staff and administrators of institutions such as clinics and hospitals. Health care providers read documents that inform them about a client's history and needs and a nurse's recommended interventions. Patients or clients read documents to learn about their health care options, home care needs, and nutrition and lifestyle choices. Administrators and staff read instructions, procedures, guidelines, reports, proposals, and policy recommendations that will enable them to make decisions and perform their functions effectively.

Your readers will expect your writing to be grounded in data, with a client's chart information and lab results clearly presented in an objective tone. You should describe your observations of a client's physical and emotional condition directly and thoroughly. You may present those observations using the first-person pronoun *I* or *we*, but be as objective as possible. Confidentiality and sensitivity to a client's background and diversity are essential.

Clients often feel anxious about their medical conditions, and many clients may not be familiar with medical terminology. When you write for clients, respect their right to understand their own medical documents. Write in plain language that is direct and easy to understand, using a minimum of technical terminology and defining such terms when it is necessary to use them. When you write for health care professionals, be precise and use relevant specialized medical terminology.

D9-b   Recognize the forms of writing in nursing.

Students in nursing school are asked to write many different kinds of papers. You might be required to write some of the following types of documents:

- statements of philosophy
- nursing practice papers
- case studies
- research papers
- literature reviews
- experiential or reflective narratives
- position papers

Statements of philosophy

To help you articulate why you want to become a nurse, your instructor may ask you to write your personal philosophy of nursing at the beginning of your professional schooling. This assignment is an opportunity to explain what principles you value, what experiences have shaped your career path, how you plan to put your principles into practice, and perhaps what specialization you are interested in pursuing.

Nursing practice papers

Assignments that ask you to apply your growing knowledge about medicine and care practices can take different forms: a nursing care plan, a concept map, or a nursing process paper. For these practice papers, you provide

- a detailed client history and a nursing diagnosis of the client's health problems
- the interventions you recommend for the client
- your rationales for the interventions
- expected outcomes for the client
- actual, observed outcomes

A concept map is an important technique that students can use to understand how to approach client care or how to sort through possible solutions to a problem. Students create a diagram that shows the connections between the possible diagnoses, the client and medical research data that could support each diagnosis, and the plans for client care that follow from each diagnosis.

Case studies

When you are asked to do a case study, you are given detailed information about a hypothetical client's health issue and are instructed to analyze the data. Case studies help you develop a global view of the many elements that make up a client's health problems and shape the health care decisions you make for the client. In a case study, you might

- interpret laboratory results
- evaluate data from a chart that a nurse on the previous shift has completed
- prioritize the client's medical needs
- determine the necessary guidelines for carrying out any required procedures (such as wound care)
- consider, with sensitivity, how the client's personal history, including language and cultural background, might inform how you interact with the client, answer questions, and respond to his or her needs

Research papers

A research paper assignment calls on you to research and report on a topic relevant to the nursing field—perhaps a particular disease, such as Alzheimer's, or an issue that challenges medical professionals, such as maintaining quality care when the downsizing of nursing staffs leads to longer, more fatiguing shifts. Typically, you are required to use as sources as many as twenty-five scholarly articles published in peer-reviewed journals in medical fields. (Peer-reviewed journals publish manuscripts only after they have been carefully reviewed anonymously by experts in the field.)

In some cases, you will be asked to formulate a research question (such as *Is the use of animal-assisted therapy effective in managing behavioral problems of clients with Alzheimer's?*) and come to a conclusion based on a review of recently published research. In other cases, you may be expected to synthesize information from a number of published articles to answer questions about a nursing practice, such as medication administration, or about a disorder, such as muscular dystrophy.

Literature reviews

Review assignments ask you to read and synthesize published work on a nursing topic. As a nursing student you will read many scholarly articles about medical conditions and nursing practices, so it is important to understand and stay current with the latest advances in the field. In a literature review, you summarize the arguments or findings of one or more journal articles or of a larger body of recent scholarship on a topic. In some cases, you may be asked more specifically to analyze the works critically, evaluating whether the findings seem justified by the data. Such an assignment may be called a *critical review*.

Experiential or reflective narratives

Some of the writing you do as a nursing student will be reflective. To begin to understand what clients are experiencing because of an illness, you might write a personal narrative about what happened to you while caring for a client or what happened to your client as he or she coped with an illness. For example, one student wrote about the increasing sense of isolation and hopelessness that an elderly woman suffered because of her late-stage glaucoma.

Position papers

In a position paper, you take a stance on a controversial issue in the field, such as whether the government should prohibit junk food commercials during children's television programming. You must support your argument with evidence from published research and show the evidence and reasoning that may support an opposing position. A good position paper makes clear why the issue is controversial and important to debate.

D9-c   Know the questions nurses ask.

Nursing students ask questions in their writing that help them effectively care for clients. You might ask questions such as the following to understand the needs of clients.

- What information should you collect each day from a client with a particular condition?
- Do the data in the client's chart indicate a normal or an abnormal status of his or her condition?

- What interventions should you take based on the diagnosis of the client's condition? Why are those interventions necessary?
- How do you care for a surgical patient with chronic pain?

D9-d Understand the kinds of evidence nurses use.

When you are writing a paper in nursing, sometimes your evidence will be quantitative (such as lab results or a client's vital signs), and sometimes it will be qualitative (such as your observations and descriptions of a client's appearance or state of mind). The following are examples of the kinds of evidence you might use:

- a client's lab test results
- data from a nurse's client chart
- research findings in a journal article
- direct observation of a client's physical or mental state

Because clients can have multiple medical problems that need to be prioritized for treatment, nurses use evidence to support more than one nursing diagnosis.

D9-e Become familiar with writing conventions in nursing.

Nurses agree on some conventions when they write.

- Nurses increasingly refer to the people in their care as "clients," not "patients."
- Evaluations and conclusions must be based on accurate and detailed information (*At the time of his diagnosis, the client had experienced a 20-lb weight loss in the previous 6 months. His CBC showed a WBC count of 32, an H & H of 13/38, and a platelet count of 34,000*).
- The first-person pronoun *I* is acceptable in reflective papers about your own experience, but you should use an objective voice in the third person for research papers, reviews, case studies, position papers, and papers describing nursing practices (*Postoperative findings: External fixation devices extend from the proximal tibia and fibular shafts of the left foot*).
- Nurses often use the passive voice in describing procedures or recording their observations (*Inflammation was observed at the site of the incision*).

- The identity of clients whose cases are discussed in writing must remain confidential (nurses often make up initials to denote a client's name).

- Direct quotation of sources is rare; instead, nurses paraphrase to demonstrate their understanding of the source material and to convey information economically.

- The APA (American Psychological Association) system of headings and subheadings helps readers see the hierarchy of sections in a paper.

D9-f Use the APA system in writing in nursing.

Writers in nursing typically use the style guidelines of the American Psychological Association (APA) for formatting their paper, for citing sources in the text of their paper, and for listing sources at the end. The APA system is set forth in the *Publication Manual of the American Psychological Association*, 6th ed. (Washington, DC: APA, 2010). (For more details, see the APA documentation sections in your handbook.)

D9-g Sample student paper: Nursing practice paper

If you are asked to write a nursing practice paper, you will need to provide a detailed client history, a nursing diagnosis of the client's health problems, the interventions you recommend to care for the client and your rationales for those interventions, and the expected and actual outcomes for your client. The following student paper was written for a nursing course that focused on clinical experience. The writer, Julie Riss, used the style guidelines of the American Psychological Association (APA) to format her paper and to cite and list her sources.

Running head: ALL AND HTN IN ONE CLIENT   1

> The header consists of a shortened title in all capital letters at the left margin and the page number at the right margin; on the title page only, the shortened title is preceded by the words "Running head" and a colon.

Acute Lymphoblastic Leukemia and Hypertension in One Client:

A Nursing Practice Paper

Julie Riss

George Mason University

> Full title, writer's name, and school halfway down the page.

> An author's note lists specific information about the course or department and can provide acknowledgments and contact information.

Author Note

This paper was prepared for Nursing 451, taught by Professor Durham. The author wishes to thank the nursing staff of Milltown General Hospital for help in understanding client care and diagnosis.

Marginal annotations indicate APA-style formatting and effective writing.

D9-g

Full title, repeated.

Headings and
subheadings, in
APA style, mark
the sections of the
report and help
readers follow the
organization.

Riss begins by
summarizing the
client's history
using information
from his chart and
her interview.

Riss respects the
client's privacy
by using only his
initials in her paper.

Riss describes her
detailed assessment
of the client, using
appropriate medical
terminology.

Acute Lymphoblastic Leukemia and Hypertension in One Client:

A Nursing Practice Paper

Historical and Physical Assessment

Physical History

E.B. is a 16-year-old white male 5'10" tall weighing 190 lb.
He was admitted to the hospital on April 14, 2006, due to decreased
platelets and a need for a PRBC transfusion. He was diagnosed in October
2005 with T-cell acute lymphoblastic leukemia (ALL), after a 2-week period
of decreased energy, decreased oral intake, easy bruising, and petechia.
The client had experienced a 20-lb weight loss in the previous 6 months.
At the time of diagnosis, his CBC showed a WBC count of 32, an H & H of
13/38, and a platelet count of 34,000. His initial chest X-ray showed an
anterior mediastinal mass. Echocardiogram showed a structurally normal
heart. He began induction chemotherapy on October 12, 2005, receiving
vincristine, 6-mercaptopurine, doxorubicin, intrathecal methotrexate,
and then high-dose methotrexate per protocol. He was diagnosed with
hypertension (HTN) due to systolic blood pressure readings consistently
ranging between 130s and 150s and was started on nifedipine. E.B. has
a history of mild ADHD, migraines, and deep vein thrombosis (DVT). He
has tolerated the induction and consolidation phases of chemotherapy
well and is now in the maintenance phase, in which he receives a daily
dose of mercaptopurine, weekly doses of methotrexate, and intermittent
doses of steroids.

Psychosocial History

There is a possibility of a depressive episode a year previously when
he would not attend school. He got into serious trouble and was sent to a
shelter for 1 month. He currently lives with his mother, father, and 14-year-
old sister.

Family History

Paternal: prostate cancer and hypertension in grandfather

Maternal: breast cancer and heart disease

Current Assessment

Client's physical exam reveals him to be alert and oriented to person,
place, and time. He communicates, though not readily. His speech and
vision are intact. He has an equal grip bilaterally and can move all

ALL AND HTN IN ONE CLIENT   3

extremities, though he is generally weak. Capillary refill is less than
2 s. His peripheral pulses are strong and equal, and he is positive for
posterior tibial and dorsalis pedis bilaterally. His lungs are clear to
auscultation, his respiratory rate is 16, and his oxygen saturation is
99% on room air. He has positive bowel sounds in all quadrants, and his
abdomen is soft, round, and nontender. He is on a regular diet, but his
appetite has been poor. Client is voiding appropriately and his urine is
clear and yellow. He appears pale and is unkempt. His skin is warm, dry,
and intact. He has alopecia as a result of chemotherapy. His mediport site
has no redness or inflammation. He appears somber and is slow to comply
with nursing instructions.

Assessment uses a neutral tone.

Medical Diagnosis #1: Acute Lymphoblastic Leukemia

Leukemia is a neoplastic disease that involves the blood-forming
tissues of the bone marrow, spleen, and lymph nodes. In leukemia the
ratio of red to white blood cells is reversed. There are approximately
2,500 cases of acute lymphoblastic leukemia (ALL) per year in the United
States, and it is the most common type of leukemia in children—it
accounts for 75%-80% of childhood leukemias. The peak age of onset
is 4 years, and it affects whites more often than blacks and males more
often than females. Risk factors include Down syndrome or genetic
disorders; exposures to ionizing radiation and certain chemicals such as
benzene; human T-cell leukemia/lymphoma virus-1; and treatment for
certain cancers.

APA allows extra space above headings when it improves readability.

ALL causes an abnormal proliferation of lymphoblasts in
the bone marrow, lymph nodes, and spleen. As the lymphoblasts
proliferate, they suppress the other hematopoietic elements in the
marrow. The leukemic cells do not function as mature cells and so do not
work as they should in the immune and inflammatory processes. Because
the growth of red blood cells and platelets is suppressed, the signs and
symptoms of the disease are infections, bleeding, pallor, bone pain,
weight loss, sore throat, fatigue, night sweats, and weakness. Treatment
involves chemotherapy, bone marrow transplant, or stem cell transplant
(LeMone & Burke, 2004).

Riss paraphrases the source and uses an APA-style in-text citation.

Medical Diagnosis #2: Hypertension

Riss demonstrates her understanding of the medical condition.

Primary hypertension in adolescence is a condition in which the blood pressure is persistently elevated to the 95th to 99th percentile for age, sex, and weight (Hockenberry, 2003). It must be elevated on three separate occasions for diagnosis to be made. Approximately 50 million people in the United States suffer from hypertension. It most often affects middle-aged and older adults and is more prevalent in black adults than in whites and Hispanics. In blacks the prevalence between males and females is equal, but in whites and Hispanics more males than females are affected. Risk factors include family history, age, race, mineral intake, obesity, insulin resistance, excess alcohol consumption, smoking, and stress. Hypertension results from sustained increases in blood volume and peripheral resistance. The increased blood volume causes an increase in cardiac output, which causes systemic arteries to vasoconstrict. This increased vascular resistance causes hypertension. Hypertension accelerates the rate of atherosclerosis, increasing the risk factor for heart disease and stroke. The workload of the heart is increased, causing ventricular hypertrophy, which increases risk for heart disease, dysrhythmias, and heart failure. Early hypertension usually exhibits no symptoms. The elevations in blood pressure are temporary at first but then progress to being permanent. A headache in the back of the head when awakening may be the only symptom. Other symptoms include blurred vision, nausea and vomiting, and nocturia. Treatment involves medications such as ACE inhibitors, diuretics, beta-adrenergic blockers, calcium channel blockers, and vasodilators as well as changes in diet, such as decreased sodium intake. An increase in physical activity is essential to aid in weight loss and to reduce stress (LeMone & Burke, 2004).

Chart Review

Active Orders

Vital signs q4h

Fall precautions

OOB as tolerated

Oximetry monitoring—continuous

ALL AND HTN IN ONE CLIENT   5

CBC with manual differential daily in am

Regular diet

Weight—daily

Strict intake and output monitoring

Type and cross match

PRBCs—2 units

Platelets—1 unit

Discharge after CBC results posttransfusion shown to MD

Rationale for Orders

  Vital signs are monitored every four hours per unit standard. In addition, the client's hypertension is an indication for close monitoring of blood pressure. He has generalized weakness, so fall precautions should be implemented. Though he is weak, ambulation is important, especially considering the client's history of DVT. A regular diet is ordered—I'm not sure why the client is not on a low-sodium diet, given his hypertension. Intake and output monitoring is standard on the unit. His hematological status needs to be carefully monitored due to his anemia and thrombocytopenia; therefore he has a CBC with manual differential done each morning. In addition, his hematological status is checked posttransfusion to see if the blood and platelets he receives increase his RBC and platelet counts. Transfused platelets survive in the body approximately 1-3 days, and the peak effect is achieved about 2 hr posttransfusion. Though platelets normally do not have to be cross-matched for blood group or type, children who receive multiple transfusions may become sensitized to a platelet group other than their own. Therefore, platelets are cross-matched with the donor's blood components. Blood and platelet transfusions may result in hemolytic, febrile, or allergic reactions, so the client is carefully monitored during the transfusion. Hospital protocol requires a set of baseline vital signs prior to transfusion vital signs. After the blood and platelets have been given, the physician is apprised of CBC results to be sure that the client's thrombocytopenia has resolved before he is discharged.

Riss uses specialized medical terminology.

Riss shows how physiology, prescribed treatments, and nursing practices are related.

ALL AND HTN IN ONE CLIENT   6

Pharmacological Interventions and Goals

Short tables, like
those in this paper,
are placed within
the text. A longer
table can be placed
on a separate page.

Medications and Effects

ondansetron hydrochloride (Zofran) 8 mg PO PRN	serotonin receptor antagonist, antiemetic—prevention of nausea and vomiting associated with chemotherapy
famotidine (Pepcid) 10 mg PO ac	H2 receptor antagonist, antiulcer agent—prevention of heartburn
nifedipine (Procardia) 30 mg PO bid	calcium channel blocker, antihypertensive—prevention of hypertension
enoxaparin sodium (Lovenox) 60 mg SQ bid	low-molecular-weight heparin derivative, anticoagulant—prevention of DVT
mercaptopurine (Purinethol) 100 mg PO qhs	antimetabolite, antineoplastic—treatment of ALL
PRBCs—2 units leukoreduced, irradiated[a]	to increase RBC count
platelets—1 unit[a]	to treat thrombocytopenia

[a]Because these products are dispensed by pharmacy, they are considered a pharmacological intervention, even though technically not medications.

Laboratory Tests and Significance

Riss presents data
in several tables for
easy reference.

Complete Blood Count (CBC)[a]

Result name	Result	Abnormal	Normal range
WBC	3.0	*	4.5-13.0
RBC	3.73	*	4.20-5.40
Hgb	11.5		11.1-15.7
Hct	32.4	*	34.0-46.0
MCV	86.8		78.0-95.0
MCH	30.7		26.0-32.0
MCHC	35.4		32.0-36.0
RDW	14.6		11.5-15.5
Platelet	98	*	140-400
MPV	8.3		7.4-10.4

[a]*Rationale:* Client's ALL diagnosis and treatment necessitate frequent monitoring of his hematological status. WBC count, RBC, and hematocrit are decreased due to chemotherapy. The platelet count is low.

ALL AND HTN IN ONE CLIENT 7

Type and Cross-Match[a]

Result name	Result
ABORH	APOS
ANTIBODY SCR INTERP	NEGATIVE

[a]*Rationale:* To determine client's blood type and to screen for antibodies.

Vital Signs Before, During, and After Blood Transfusion[a]

Vital signs	Time	BP	Pulse	Resp	Temp (oral)
Pre	1705	113/74	92	18	98.7
15 min	1720	118/74	104	12	98.3
30 min	1735	121/74	96	16	99.3
45 min	1750	129/76	101	16	99.3
Post	1805	108/59	99	15	98.9

[a]*Rationale:* To monitor for reaction.

Nursing Diagnosis #1:
Injury, Risk for, Related to Decreased Platelet
Count and Administration of Lovenox

Desired Outcome: Client will remain free of injury.

Interventions

Monitor vital signs q4h

Assess for manifestations of bleeding such as

- Skin and mucous membranes for petechiae, ecchymoses, and hematoma formation
- Gums and nasal membranes for bleeding
- Overt or occult blood in stool or urine
- Neurologic changes

Provide sponge to clean gums and teeth

Apply pressure to puncture sites for 3-5 min

Avoid invasive procedures when possible

Administer stool softeners as prescribed

Implement fall precautions

Monitor lab values for platelets

Administer platelets as prescribed

Measurable Outcomes

Mediport site will remain intact with no signs of bleeding.

Riss prioritizes her diagnoses and recommended interventions and gives a detailed description and rationales for each.

ALL AND HTN IN ONE CLIENT ,   8

Urine and stool will remain free of blood.

Lab values for anticoagulant therapy will remain in desired range.

Platelet count will remain in normal range.

Client Teaching

Instruct client to avoid forcefully blowing nose, straining to have a bowel
movement, and forceful coughing or sneezing, all of which increase
the risk for external and internal bleeding

Discharge Planning

Instruct client to monitor for signs of decreased platelet count such as easy
bruising, petechiae, or inappropriate bleeding

Riss uses specific
examples.

Nursing Diagnosis #2:

Infection, Risk for, Related to Depressed Body Defenses

Desired Outcome: Client will remain free of infection.

Interventions

Screen all visitors and staff for signs of infection to minimize exposure to
infectious agents

Use aseptic technique for all procedures

Monitor temperature to detect possible infection

Evaluate client for potential sites of infection: needle punctures, mucosal
ulcerations

Provide nutritionally complete meals to support the body's natural
defenses

Monitor lab values for CBC

Administer G-CSF if prescribed

Measurable Outcomes

Mediport site will remain free of erythema, purulent drainage, odor, and
edema.

Client will remain afebrile.

Client Teaching

Instruct client and caregivers in correct hand-washing technique

Discharge Planning

Instruct client and caregivers to avoid live attenuated virus
vaccines

Instruct client to avoid large crowds

ALL AND HTN IN ONE CLIENT   9

Nursing Diagnosis #3:
Noncompliance, Related to HTN, as Evidenced by Lack of
Consistent Medication Regimen and Adherence to Dietary Plan

Desired Outcome: Client will follow treatment plan.

Interventions

Inquire about reasons for noncompliance

Listen openly and without judgment

Evaluate knowledge of HTN, its long-term effects, and treatment

Arrange for nutritional consult with dietitian

Measurable Outcomes

Client will take medication as prescribed.

Client's systolic blood pressure will remain in normal range.

Client Teaching

Instruct on medication regimen: appropriate administration and potential
    adverse effects

Provide information on hypertension and its treatment

Discharge Planning

Provide prescriptions

Nursing Diagnosis #4:
Health Maintenance, Ineffective, Related to
Unhealthy Lifestyle and Behaviors

Desired Outcome: Client will make changes in lifestyle.

Interventions

Assist in identifying behaviors that contribute to hypertension

Assist in developing a realistic health maintenance plan including modifying
    risk factors such as exercise, diet, and stress

Help client and family identify strengths and weaknesses in maintaining
    health

Measurable Outcomes

Client will verbalize ways to control his hypertension.

Client will identify methods to relieve stress.

Discharge Planning

Provide information on possible exercise programs

ALL AND HTN IN ONE CLIENT   10

Analysis

In the case of E.B., there are two separate disease processes
at work—ALL and HTN. The ALL is the most immediately pressing of
the two and is indirectly responsible for the client's current
hospitalization. The chemotherapy treatment for his leukemia has caused
thrombocytopenia. This condition places him at high risk for hemorrhage.
The anticoagulant therapy for DVT increases this risk even further, not
only because it may cause bleeding complications, but because in itself it
may cause thrombocytopenia. Therefore, it is imperative to raise his
platelet count as quickly as possible. Surprisingly, there were no lab
tests ordered to determine his PT and INR, both of which are monitored
when a client is on anticoagulant therapy. As his CBC demonstrates, not
only is his platelet count low, but his red blood cells are decreased.
That is why his physician ordered a transfusion of both PRBCs and
platelets.

In terms of E.B.'s diagnosis of HTN, he has a positive family
history, which is a major risk factor for developing the disease. Excess
weight is also a risk factor, and the client has a history of obesity as well.
Because exercise is an important factor in managing the excess weight
and stress associated with the disease, his leukemia and the chemotherapy
treatments aimed at curing E.B.'s leukemia actually negatively affect his
ability to manage the hypertension: He is often too weak and fatigued
to participate in much physical activity. Additionally, the steroids have
resulted in added weight gain, increasing instead of decreasing the
problem. To date, the client has failed to maintain a favorable diet
regimen.

E.B.'s family circumstances must be taken into consideration when
managing his treatment. Though he resides with both parents, there is
some question as to the support and consistency of care he receives.
He often appears very unkempt and is at times noncompliant with his
hypertension medication. Due to his parents' inability to care for a central
venous line (CVL) at home, he has a mediport that can be accessed as
needed but requires care. On a positive note, the father is aware of their
limitations and tries to work with the staff to make sure that E.B.'s ALL is
managed appropriately.

ALL AND HTN IN ONE CLIENT   11

                            References

Hockenberry, M. (2003). *Wong's nursing care of infants and children.*
     St. Louis, MO: Mosby.

LeMone, P., & Burke, K. (2004). *Medical surgical nursing: Critical thinking in*
     client care. Upper Saddle River, NJ: Pearson Education.

Riss provides a reference list for sources she cited in her paper. The list is formatted in APA style.

D10   Writing in psychology

Psychologists write with various purposes in mind. They frequently publish articles about their research or present their work at professional conferences. They write proposals to convince funding agencies to award grants for their research. Sometimes psychologists write to influence the opinions held by the public or by decision makers in government, lending their expertise to discussions on issues such as the effects of racism, the challenges of aging, or children's mental health. Psychologists may write analyses for newspaper and magazine opinion pages as well as policy recommendations and advocacy statements.

D10-a   Determine your audience and their needs in psychology.

Psychologists write for researchers, psychotherapists, teachers, students, clients, and sometimes members of the government or business community and the general public. Researchers or clinical psychologists may read to find out the results of an experiment, the analysis of new data, or information supporting or critiquing a theory. This information may be useful to readers in developing new research projects or providing services to their clients. Students read to learn about major concepts in the field. Researchers, teachers, and students expect data and findings to be communicated thoroughly in words and in graphics such as diagrams, tables, charts, and graphs. People working in government or academic settings may need information and support for decisions about funding proposed research projects.

In all cases, your readers will expect your writing to be completely objective and to present information as clearly as possible. When you are writing in psychology, you should make thorough use of others' research in the field to demonstrate your credibility. Readers are interested more in empirical data that can be presented quantitatively than in statements from experts. Qualitative information in the form of direct observations and statements from research subjects can help readers understand your conclusions or recommendations.

Your readers will appreciate your precise use of words and a scientific stance with an objective tone. When writing for clients of psychiatric or psychotherapy services, use straightforward language that respects the clients and their right to understand their conditions and needs. Such clients will also expect confidentiality and respect for diversity.

D10-b Recognize the forms of writing in psychology.

When you take courses in psychology, you may be asked to write any of the following:

- literature reviews
- research papers
- theoretical papers
- poster presentations

Literature reviews

You will likely write review papers early in your course work. In a review paper, you report on and evaluate the research that has been published in the field about a particular topic. A literature review does not merely summarize researchers' findings but argues a position with evidence that you assemble from the empirical (that is, experiment-based) studies that you review.

Sometimes a literature review stands alone as a paper, such as a survey of findings from research performed in the past century on what causes loss of memory in old age. In some cases, you will be asked to write a critical review, in which you will analyze the methods and inter-pretations of data in one or more journal articles. More often you will write a literature review as an introduction to a larger piece of writing, such as a report of your own empirical study. In that case, the literature review surveys previously published findings relevant to the question that your study investigates.

Research papers

When instructors refer to *research papers*, they may have different assignments in mind. A research paper might present your synthe-sis of many sources of information about, say, emotional responses to music. Your purpose would be to demonstrate your understanding of research findings and the ongoing debates emerging from researchers' investigations.

A research paper might also be a report on the results of an experi-ment you've conducted and on your interpretation of those results; in this case, your research paper would be an empirical study. A research paper might also relate your interpretations to what others in the field have concluded from their own experiments. Like other scientists, psychologists publish research papers in journals after the papers have undergone rigorous and impartial review by other psychologists (called *peer review*) to make sure that the scientific process used by the researchers is sound.

Whether published in a journal or written for a college course, research papers based on original experiments have the following standard elements:

- the question you set out to research and why your question is important
- a review of research relevant to your question
- your hypotheses (tentative, plausible answers to the research question that your experiment will test) and your predictions that follow from the hypotheses
- the method you used to conduct your experiment
- the results from the experiment
- your analysis of those results

Writers of research reports also use tables and figures to present experimental data in easy-to-grasp visual form.

Theoretical papers

Psychologists often write theoretical papers in which they propose their own theories or extend existing theories about a research problem in the field. For example, in one journal article, a psychologist argues that the field needs to combine attachment theory and social network theory to understand child and adolescent development.

If you are asked to write a theoretical paper for a course, you will be expected to support the theory you propose by pointing to evidence and counterevidence from the literature in the field, to compare your theory with other theories, and possibly to suggest experiments that could test your theory.

Poster presentations

At professional gatherings such as annual conventions, psychologists have the opportunity to present their work in the form of a poster rather than as a formal talk. Conference attendees approach presenters in an exhibit area to talk about the presenters' research, which the posters concisely summarize. A poster typically features an introduction to the project, the method, information about the research or the subjects of an experiment, the results, and the presenter's conclusions.

Poster presentations also feature graphs and tables since it is important to convey information to conference attendees quickly and concisely as they walk through the exhibit area. An effective poster presentation will encourage the audience to ask questions and carry on an informal conversation with the presenter.

Your instructor may ask you to create a poster presentation about an experiment you or other researchers have conducted both to help you understand complex concepts and to practice your communication skills.

NOTE: Some presenters use presentation software to create a slide show that they can click through for a small audience or project on a screen for a larger group. Presenters generally include the same kinds of information in slide presentations as they do in poster presentations.

D10-c Know the questions psychologists ask.

Psychologists generally investigate human behavior and perceptions. Their questions range widely across the different specializations that make up the field, such as animal cognition, personality, social interactions, and infant development, to name a few. The following are questions that specialists in psychology might ask.

- What personality characteristics might affect employees' personal use of work computers?
- When adult learners return to school, what is the impact on their families and working lives?
- Do variations in cerebral blood flow in different areas of the brain predict variations in performance of different imagery tasks?

D10-d Understand the kinds of evidence psychologists use.

To back up their conclusions, psychologists look for evidence in case studies and the results of experiments. They do not use expert opinion as evidence; direct quotations of what other psychologists have written are rare in psychology papers. Instead, papers focus on data (the results of experiments) and on the analysis of the results that the writer has collected.

Depending on their specialization, psychologists may ask questions that require quantitative or qualitative evidence. Quantitative evidence involves numerical measurement; qualitative evidence involves examples and illustrations.

- Quantitative evidence might be facts and statistics: *Regional cerebral blood flow in a total of 26 areas predicted performance, and 20 of these areas predicted performance only in a single task. In a study on what motivates adolescents to quit smoking, 44.7% of the participants reported that they wanted to quit because their parents wanted them to.* Or it might be results of original experiments: *Fraudulent excuse scores were correlated with cheating scores (r = .37, n = 211, p < .0001).*

- Qualitative evidence might be descriptions of interviews or statements of the researcher's observations: *Many of the respondents believed that girls' tendency either to address indirectly or to avoid conflict was supported by adults, who expected them to be* ladylike; *when asked to define this term, they used such descriptors as "mature" and "calm."*

D10-e   Become familiar with writing conventions in psychology.

Psychologists use straightforward and concise language and depend on special terms to explain their findings.

- Specialized vocabulary may include terms such as *methods, results, double-blind study, social identity perspective,* and *nonverbal emotions.*

- Often researchers use specific, technical definitions of terms that nonspecialists use differently. For example, if a psychologist asks whether adults with eating disorders are "depressed," the term refers to a specific mental disorder, not to a general mood of sadness.

- When reporting conclusions, writers in psychology use the past tense (*Berkowitz found*) or the present perfect tense (*Berkowitz has found*). When discussing results, they use the present tense (*The results confirm*). They avoid using subjective expressions like *I think* and *I feel.*

D10-f   Use the APA system in writing in psychology.

Writers in psychology typically use the style guidelines of the American Psychological Association (APA) for formatting their papers, for citing sources in the text of their papers, and for listing sources at the end. The APA system is set forth in the *Publication Manual of the American Psychological Association*, 6th ed. (Washington, DC: APA, 2010). (For more details, see the APA documentation sections in your handbook.)

D10-g Sample student paper: Literature review (excerpt)

A psychology literature review assignment usually asks you both to survey published research on a topic in the field and to argue your own position with evidence that you assemble from your survey. The student paper excerpted beginning on the next page was written for a second-year developmental psychology course. The student, Valerie Charat, used the style guidelines of the American Psychological Association (APA) to format her paper and to cite and list her sources.

The header consists of a shortened title in all capital letters at the left margin and the page number at the right margin; on the title page only, the shortened title is preceded by the words "Running head" and a colon.

Running head: ADHD IN BOYS VS. GIRLS   1

Full title, writer's name, and school halfway down the page.

Always out of Their Seats (and Fighting):

Why Are Boys Diagnosed With ADHD More Often Than Girls?

Valerie Charat

Harvard University

An author's note lists specific information about the course or department and can provide acknowledgments and contact information.

Author Note

This paper was prepared for Psychology 1806, taught by Professor Korfine.

Marginal annotations indicate APA-style formatting and effective writing.

ADHD IN BOYS VS. GIRLS   2

Abstract

Until the early 1990s, most research on attention deficit hyperactivity disorder (ADHD) focused on boys and did not explore possible gender differences. Recent studies have suggested that gender differences do exist and are caused by personality differences between boys and girls, by gender bias in referring teachers and clinicians, or by the diagnostic procedures themselves. But the most likely reason is that ADHD is often comorbid—that is, it coexists with other behavior disorders that are not diagnosed properly and that do exhibit gender differences. This paper first considers studies of gender differences only in ADHD and then looks at studies of gender differences when ADHD occurs with comorbid disorders. Future research must focus more specifically on how gender differences are influenced by factors such as referrals, family history, and comorbid conditions.

Keywords: ADHD, hyperactivity, attention deficit, gender differences, comorbid conditions

Abstract, a 100-to-150-word overview of the paper, appears on a separate page.

ADHD IN BOYS VS. GIRLS   3

Full title, repeated.

Charat gives
abbreviations
in parentheses
the first time she
uses common
psychology terms.

Introduction
provides
background to
the topic and
establishes why a
literature review on
ADHD is necessary.

Thesis states what
Charat will argue
by describing and
analyzing the
sources she has
reviewed.

Charat uses APA
style to cite her
sources. Two
sources in one
parenthetical
citation are
separated with a
semicolon.

Headings, centered,
divide the paper
into two main
sections.

Always out of Their Seats (and Fighting):

Why Are Boys Diagnosed With ADHD More Often Than Girls?

Attention deficit hyperactivity disorder (ADHD) is a commonly diagnosed disorder in children that affects social, academic, or occupational functioning. As the name suggests, its hallmark characteristics are hyperactivity and lack of attention as well as impulsive behavior. For decades, studies have focused on the causes, expression, prevalence, and outcome of the disorder, but until recently very little research investigated gender differences. In fact, until the early 1990s most research focused exclusively on boys (Brown, Madan-Swain, & Baldwin, 1991), perhaps because many more boys than girls are diagnosed with ADHD. Researchers have speculated on the possible explanations for the disparity, citing reasons such as true sex differences in the manifestation of the disorder's symptoms, gender biases in those who refer children to clinicians, and possibly even the diagnostic procedures themselves (Gaub & Carlson, 1997). But the most persuasive reason is that ADHD is often a comorbid condition—that is, it coexists with other behavior disorders that are not diagnosed properly and that do exhibit gender differences.

It has been suggested that in the United States children are often misdiagnosed as having ADHD when they actually suffer from a behavior disorder such as conduct disorder (CD) or a combination of ADHD and another behavior disorder (Disney, Elkins, McGue, & Iancono, 1999; Lilienfeld & Waldman, 1990). Conduct disorder is characterized by negative and criminal behavior in children and is highly correlated with adult diagnoses of antisocial personality disorder (ASPD). This paper first considers research that has dealt only with gender difference in the occurrence of ADHD and then looks at research that has studied the condition along with other behavior disorders.

Gender Differences in Studies of ADHD

Most of the research on ADHD has lacked a comparative component. Throughout the 1970s and 1980s, most research focused only on boys. If girls were included, it was often in such low numbers that gender-based comparisons were unwarranted (Gaub & Carlson, 1997). One of the least debated differences is the dissimilarity in male and female prevalence

ADHD IN BOYS VS. GIRLS　　　　　　　　　　　　　4

rates. Some studies have claimed a 3:1 ratio of boys with ADHD to girls with ADHD (American Psychiatric Association, 1987), while others have cited ratios as high as 9:1 (Brown et al., 1991). The differences in prevalence have been attributed to a variety of causes, one of which is that girls may have more internalized symptoms and may be overlooked in ADHD diagnoses (Brown et al., 1991).

A study conducted by Breen (1989) sought to test the differences in cognition, behavior, and academic functioning for boys and girls. Past research had indicated that boys with ADHD showed more aggressive behavior while girls showed more learning problems, but the results were often conflicting. To clarify the existing information, Breen conducted a study on 39 children aged 6 to 11, from a group of children referred to a pediatric psychology clinic. All subjects were white, with varying socioeconomic status. He broke the subjects into three groups: boys with ADHD, girls with ADHD, and a control group of girls without any psychiatric or family history of behavioral or emotional problems. Each group was given a battery of tests to assess cognitive functioning. All children were also observed in a playroom while they worked math problems, and all were coded for a variety of behaviors including fidgeting, vocalizing, being out of their seats, and so on.

The results showed that while both groups with ADHD performed nearly equally across most measures, ADHD boys were generally viewed as more deviant than normal girls. Girls with ADHD were closer behaviorally to girls in the control group than to ADHD boys. This finding indicates that it may be difficult to distinguish girls with ADHD from girls without the disorder based solely on behavior. This conclusion was corroborated by the later finding (Brown et al., 1991) that girls with ADHD are often not clinically referred unless they demonstrate a more severe form of the disorder than boys do. A contradictory finding (Breen, 1989) was that ADHD boys and girls displayed rates of disruptive behavior that were not significantly different from each other, although Breen did not indicate what forms the disruptive behavior took and whether the girls were less aggressive than the boys. But as Brown et al. (1991) later pointed out, it was easier to differentiate ADHD in externalized behaviors—aggression, inattention, and overactivity—than in internalized behaviors—depression,

---

Charat summarizes key research findings about the paper's central question.

A signal phrase names the author and gives the date of the source in parentheses.

Charat examines an important study in detail. She summarizes experimental methods used by researchers.

Charat uses the specialized language of the field.

Source first mentioned on page 3. In subsequent citations, for a source with three to five authors "et al." is used after the first author's name in the text and in parentheses.

anxiety, and withdrawal. It is striking, however, that the distinction in Breen's study was clearer not between boys and girls but between girls with and girls without ADHD. Breen concluded that differences between boys and girls with the disorder do not seem significant.

A few drawbacks to Breen's study include a lack of screening for comorbid conduct disorders, which were no doubt present in some of the subjects. The small sample size could have hindered the results, with only 13 subjects in each group. Another limitation is the small cross section: All subjects were white and clinically referred. Therefore, the findings cannot be generalized to a nonclinical, racially diverse population. Finally, the lack of male controls is surprising, given the usual trend to overrepresent boys when studying ADHD. A reasonable comparison would have been between girls with ADHD and boys in a control group to see if the girls' range of antisocial behavior was beyond that of control boys.

Another study (Maughan, Pickles, Hagell, Rutter, & Yule, 1996) investigated the association between reading problems and antisocial behavior. The researchers cited a connection that had previously been made (Hinshaw, 1992, as cited in Maughan et al., 1996) between antisocial behavior and underachievement in early childhood, while aggression and antisocial behavior became salient in later years. Maughan et al. looked specifically at reading because research has shown that children who develop reading problems have higher rates of behavioral problems even before they learn to read (Jorm, Share, Matthews, & Mclean, 1986). It had also been shown that reading problems can affect behavioral development (Pianta & Caldwell, 1992, as cited in Maughan et al., 1996). However, since most studies had been done with boys, the researchers also compared gender differences.

Subjects were selected from a previously conducted study in a population of children who were 10 years old in 1970. The majority were British-born Caucasians of low socioeconomic status. The analysis used two subsamples, one with poor reading scores, the other a randomly sampled control group with average IQ and no reading difficulties. Poor readers were rated as either "backward" or "retarded." The subjects in the backward group were 28 months below average in reading level for their age and IQ. At age 10, children had received psychometric testing, and the study

---

Annotations in margin:

Charat analyzes the study's shortcomings.

Topic sentence states paragraph's main point.

An indirect source (work quoted in another source) is indicated with the words "as cited in."

An ampersand separates the authors' names in parentheses.

Charat describes the study's methods in detail.

ADHD IN BOYS VS. GIRLS   6

accounted for parental occupation, the child's government benefits status, and the ranking of the child's state school in terms of economic adversity. There were follow-ups at ages 14, 17, and early 20s.

Poor readers demonstrated high rates of behavior problems by age 10. About 40% of the girls and almost 50% of the boys in the retarded reading group exhibited antisocial behavior at age 10. Interestingly, reading-retarded girls showed high rates of conduct problems, while the boys did not. Also, among girls there were much higher rates of antisocial behavior in the lowest socioeconomic category than in slightly higher socioeconomic categories. In boys, the differences were not as pronounced. For boys, poor performance in school was the only predictor of antisocial behavior, while for girls poor school performance and reading level were predictors. This finding suggests that for boys, learning difficulties do not increase the risk of behavior problems, while for girls they do. Inattentiveness and overactivity were also related to reading problems and were highly related to antisocial behavior. When inattentiveness and overactivity were factored in, there were no direct links between reading difficulties and antisocial behavior. This absent connection means that reading problems do not cause antisocial behavior. It is when they cannot pay attention or sit long enough to read that both boys and girls exhibit elevated rates of antisocial behavior.

By age 14, girls still showed a significant correlation between reading problems and antisocial behavior, while boys showed no association. In early adulthood (ages 17 and early 20s), criminality, alcohol problems, aggression, and personality disorders were found in low rates in girls. In the sample of girls interviewed in their 20s, 1.9% had juvenile offense records and 5.4% had records of adult crime. In boys, poor readers did not show any significant rates of antisocial personality disorders.

The study had several drawbacks. Subject responses at follow-up periods were not uniformly gathered, and the lack of analysis of female juvenile offenders made it harder to understand the results in terms of gender differences and antisocial behavior. The sample consisted only of inner-city children of low socioeconomic status because they had higher rates of reading difficulty than other children. But because economic adversity was found to be a predictor for poor conduct in girls, this group

In APA style, the numbers 10 and above are expressed in numerals; percentages are expressed in numbers with a percent symbol.

After presenting the study's findings, Charat analyzes the study's weaknesses.

ADHD IN BOYS VS. GIRLS   7

of subjects may have contained a disproportionate number of female subjects with more severe antisocial behavior.

Of particular interest was that for girls but not for boys, reading level and low socioeconomic status predicted antisocial behavior. However, when the children were followed into adulthood, the females who had originally displayed antisocial behavior did not show elevated rates of juvenile offenses or adult crime. Perhaps the results indicate that girls with antisocial and hyperactive behavior in childhood are different from boys in that they are responding to passing learning impairments rather than permanent personality problems. Or girls may have continued to have ADHD, but with internalized rather than externalized symptoms. Another possibility is that the girls had more severe forms of ADHD because of sampling bias for socioeconomic status but that they eventually grew out of the disorder in adolescence while the boys did not.

Another study (Brown et al., 1991) looked specifically at the cognitive and academic performance of children with ADHD and compared internalizing versus externalizing features of the disorder across genders. As in Breen (1989), Brown et al. (1991) found there were few gender differences on measures of attention, concentration, and distractibility. However, some significant differences were found. Parent and teacher ratings of internalizing and externalizing characteristics described boys as more aggressive and girls as more unpopular. Girls were also more commonly held back one or two grades, a finding the researchers interpreted as evidence of female academic difficulties and possible neurological disorders or impairments. This would correlate with the findings of Maughan et al. (1996) of an association between reading impairment and antisocial behaviors in ADHD girls. However, the data must also be regarded cautiously. Brown et al. did not use a control group and thus did not have a standard by which to measure the differences. Any implication of a neurological impairment in females with ADHD should be viewed skeptically. The historical perception of women as the weaker or more defective sex should make any researcher reluctant to postulate . . .

[Charat continues to describe and analyze researchers' studies and findings.]

Charat speculates on possible explanations for the results of the study.

If a source is cited in the text of the paragraph, only the authors' names are given when the source is cited later in the text of the same paragraph. (The date is required in all parenthetical citations.)

ADHD IN BOYS VS. GIRLS   11

Conclusion

Although the studies presented here are filled with flaws and contradictory findings, they have a unifying thread. Through direct findings or indirect lack of information, all suggest that the higher rate of male diagnoses of ADHD does not necessarily mean that the disorder actually occurs in boys more often than in girls. Although boys are more commonly diagnosed, this phenomenon could reflect a long-standing history of misperceptions. Since hyperactive and inattentive boys are also often aggressive and disruptive, girls who do not demonstrate similar behaviors may be overlooked.

It is important to reevaluate the way boys and girls are observed and understood when attention and hyperactivity are being assessed. Males and females may display different behaviors, and parents and teachers may interpret their behaviors differently. But when rated by trained researchers, boys and girls identified as having ADHD are rated similarly. However, it is easier to identify externalizing, aggressive behavior than it is to identify internalizing behavior, and this difference may be one of the main factors at the root of the perceived gender differences in the prevalence of ADHD. There is not enough concrete evidence to rule out the possibility that a gender difference does exist, regardless of the fact that boys and girls seem to show equal rates and degrees of symptoms. Until more studies look at population samples, exclude conduct disorders, and take into account possible differences in the ways the symptoms are manifested, it is impossible to conclude that gender differences are the result of social and clinical biases and stereotypes. Further research on genetics and familial rates of the disorder are also necessary to help clarify the relationship between adult antisocial personality disorder and ADHD. Also, until a clear distinction is made between conduct disorder and ADHD, not only in the text of the *DSM-IV* but also in the minds of laypeople and clinicians, it will be difficult to separate children with comorbid disorder and those without it and to assess gender differences as well.

Conclusion presents a synthesis of the paper's points.

Charat raises questions about the research she reviews but adopts a balanced tone in summarizing the sources.

Charat suggests areas for future research.

Conclusion affirms the necessity of continuing investigation.

List of references
begins on a new
page. The first line
of an entry is at
the left margin;
subsequent lines
indent ½".

If an online source
has a DOI (digital
object identifier),
no URL is given.

A work with up to
seven authors lists
all authors' names.
A work with more
than seven authors
lists the first six
followed by three
ellipsis dots and the
last author's name.

List is alphabetized
by authors' last
names. All authors'
names are inverted;
an ampersand
separates the last
two authors.

                              References

American Psychiatric Association. (1987). *Diagnostic and statistical manual*
        of mental disorders (3rd ed., rev.). Washington, DC: Author.

American Psychiatric Association. (1994). *Diagnostic and statistical manual*
        of mental disorders (4th ed.). Washington, DC: Author.

Breen, M. J. (1989). Cognitive and behavioral differences in AdHD boys
        and girls. *Journal of Child Psychology and Psychiatry, 30,* 711-716.
        doi:10.1111/j.1469-7610.1989.tb00783.x

Breen, M. J., & Altepeter, T. S. (1990). Situational variability in boys and
        girls identified as ADHD. *Journal of Clinical Psychology, 46,* 486-490.

Brown, R. T., Madan-Swain, A., & Baldwin, K. (1991). Gender differences in
        a clinic-referred sample of attention-deficit-disordered children. *Child*
        Psychiatry and Human Development, 22, 111-127.

Disney, E. R., Elkins, J. J., McGue, M., & Iancono, W. G. (1999). Effects of
        ADHD, conduct disorder, and gender on substance use and abuse in
        adolescence. *American Journal of Psychiatry, 156,* 1515-1521.

Faraone, S. V., Biederman, J., Chen, W. J., Milberger, S., Warburton, R.,
        & Tsuang, M. T. (1995). Genetic heterogeneity in attention-deficit
        hyperactivity disorder (ADHD): Gender, psychiatric comorbidity, and
        maternal ADHD. *Journal of Abnormal Psychology, 104,* 334-345.

Gaub, M., & Carlson, C. L. (1997). Gender differences in ADHD: A meta-
        analysis and critical review. *Journal of the American Academy of Child*
        and Adolescent Psychiatry, 36, 1036-1045.

Jorm, A. F., Share, D. L., Matthews, R., & Mclean, R. (1986). Behaviour
        problems in specific reading retarded and general reading backward
        children: A longitudinal study. *Journal of Child Psychology and*
        Psychiatry, 27, 33-43. doi:10.1111/j.1469-7610.1986.tb00619.x

Lahey, B. B., Piacentini, J. C., McBurnett, K., Stone, P., Hartdagen, S., &
        Hynd, G. (1988). Psychopathology in the parents of children with
        conduct disorder and hyperactivity. *Journal of the American Academy*
        of Child and Adolescent Psychiatry, 27, 163-170.

Lilienfeld, S. O., & Waldman, I. D. (1990). The relation between childhood
        attention-deficit hyperactivity disorder and adult antisocial behavior
        reexamined: The problem of heterogeneity. *Clinical Psychology Review,*
        10, 699-725.

Maughan, B., Pickles, A., Hagell, A., Rutter, M., & Yule, W. (1996).
    Reading problems and antisocial behavior: Developmental trends in
    comorbidity. *Journal of Child Psychology and Psychiatry, 37*, 405-418.
    doi:10.1111/j.1469-7610.1996.tb01421.x

Oltmanns, T. F., & Emery, R. E. (1998). Psychological disorders of
    childhood. In *Abnormal psychology* (2nd ed., pp. 572-607). Upper
    Saddle River, NJ: Prentice Hall.

Sprock, J., Blashfield, R. K., & Smith, B. (1990). Gender weighting of
    DSM-III-R personality disorder criteria. *American Journal of
    Psychiatry, 147*, 586-590.

Index

This is the index for Tab D only. For the
handbook's main index, see the I (Index) tab.

This is the index for Tab D only. For the handbook's main index, see the I (Index) tab.

This is the index for Tab D only. For the handbook's main index, see the I (Index) tab.

This is the index for Tab D only. For the handbook's main index, see the I (Index) tab.